JESUS–

FINAL AUTHORITY ON MARRIAGE AND SAME-SEX UNIONS

WILLIAM E. BERG

LUTHERAN
COLPORTAGE
SERVICE, INC.

Published by Lutheran Colportage Service, Inc.,
Minneapolis, Minnesota

Scripture quotations, unless otherwise noted,
are taken from the *Revised Standard Version* of the Bible,
copyright © 1946, 1952, 1971 by the Division of Christian
Education of the National Council of Churches
of Christ in the USA. Used by permission.

Scripture quotations marked TLB are taken
from *The Living Bible*, copyright © 1971.
Used by permission of Tyndale House Publishers, Inc.,
Wheaton, Illinois 60189. All rights reserved.

Scripture quotations marked KJV are taken from
the *King James Version* of the Bible.

Scripture quotations marked NKJV are taken from
The Holy Bible, New King James Version, copyright ©
1982 by Thomas Nelson, Inc. Used by permission.

Scripture quotation marked GNT is taken from
the *Good News Translation,* copyright © 1992,
American Bible Society. Used by permission.

Scripture quotations marked NEB are taken from
The New English Bible, copyright © 1989 by
Oxford University Press and Cambridge
University Press. Used by permission.

Printed by Sentinel Printing, St. Cloud, Minnesota

Front Cover Photo-Courtesy of Arland Erickson

ISBN 0-9715299-4-9

Table of Contents

Dedication

This book is dedicated to the editors. They are Karen Conrad Balmer, Anne Carlson, Jon Carlson, Katie Carlson, Dr. Theodore E. Conrad, Don and Karin Goodell, Glenn Knoblauch, Katherine Krause and Carol Smith. These blessed partners and co-workers know that rewriting is an author's biggest challenge. They also know that rereading and correcting are a high price that must be paid for the creation of a book. It is a high price in terms of the expenditure of energy, time and thought by many persons. For their dedication and encouragement in the long journey toward publication, and for the high inspiration of working with them in our Lord's service, I shall forever be grateful.

Foreword

Despite its title, this book is not, first and foremost, about marriage and same-sex unions. It is about Jesus and His Divine Design. The first three words of this book are "Jesus–Final Authority". This is an affirmation of faith. The last three words of this book are "in Christ Jesus". This is an expression of trust. This book begins with a crisis–the crisis of Christology. It seeks to answer the question, "Who is Jesus?" The last chapter of the book highlights a theology of hope, centered in Jesus who is Lord of the Church.

This is a "reflection book". It seeks to reflect the teachings of Jesus on a controversial issue facing the Church today.

For some in the Church, the issue of same-sex unions is a "justice issue". Are not all persons, whether of homosexual or heterosexual orientation, to be treated equally? But it is more than a human justice issue. It is a Divine Justice issue. We listen to the Divine Judge:

"I can do nothing on my own authority;
as I hear, I judge; and my judgment is just,
because I seek not my own will but the will of him who sent me."
JOHN 5:30

Divine Justice always comes with Divine Mercy. God's love for all of us sinners is a central theme:

"But God shows his love for us
in that while we were yet sinners Christ died for us."
ROMANS 5:8

There are many controversial issues on human sexuality. Can we hope for unity in the midst of diversity? Indeed, we can if we find our unity in Jesus. St. Paul admonishes us in Ephesians 4:1-3:

"I therefore, a prisoner for the Lord,
beg you to lead a life worthy of the calling to which you have been
called, with all lowliness and meekness, with patience,

forbearing one another in love,
eager to maintain the unity of the Spirit in the bond of peace."

The need for compassion is one of the concerns of the Church today. Compassion means to "suffer with" which means that suffering persons are involved. But to understand the meaning of compassion, we need to think of the passion of Jesus:

"For to this you have been called,
because Christ also suffered for you, leaving you an example,
that you should follow in his steps."
I PETER 2:21

All of the highest values that we cherish in the Church are centered in a Person. Freedom is to be found in the great Liberator who sets us free from bondage to sin and self. Peace is to be found in the Prince of Peace. We find justice in the Righteous Judge. We cannot live on principles, however high they might be.

I am reminded of the story of a little girl who was crying for her mother. A friend said to her, "I cannot find your mother, but I will give you the principles of motherhood." Would a principle dry the little girl's tears? No. For all of us, each lost and hurting in our own way, a Person has come in Jesus Christ. It is my prayer that this book will encourage us to practice the Presence of Christ in the midst of our questions.

In Chapter 8 of this book, I reveal myself to be an incurable optimist. Yes, optimistic about the Church and praising God for all the mighty works of our Lord in His Church. However, I sense a troubling tendency in the Church today. It is not to reject the gospel of Jesus Christ outright, but to reduce His message so that it will fit into our human image and likeness. Someone has said, **"It is easier to change scripture than to change behavior."**

My first book entitled, *Show Me the Way to Go Home, Journey to the Promised Land*, proclaims Jesus, according to His own words, as "the Way, the Truth and the Life." In this book also, Jesus is the Center of the message. We must be careful to lift up Jesus. He said in His word:

"and I, when I am lifted up from the earth,
will draw all men to myself."
JOHN 12:32

At my age of 94, priorities become a major concern. Inevitably, there is not too much time for ministry in this world. Each day I am involved in visitation and friendship evangelism in an apartment and care center. I am still serving on the international and national boards of the Christian Ashram founded by my spiritual mentor, E. Stanley Jones. I am involved in several Bible studies each week and also in mission and evangelism committees. Ministry with my family is a major priority. Thus the question comes, "Why spend two years on this difficult and demanding assignment?" And "Why enter into a very controversial issue, especially when I have good friends whom I respect who take an opposite view from mine regarding the blessing of same-sex unions?" Reassuring words from the Bible have kept me going:

"I will instruct you and teach you the way you should go;
I will counsel you with my eye upon you."
PSALM 32:8

"Trust in the Lord with all your heart,
and lean not on your own understanding.
In all your ways acknowledge Him,
and He shall direct your paths."
PROVERBS 3:5,6 (NKJV)

"'For I know the plans I have for you', says the Lord.
'They are plans for good and not for evil,
to give you a future and a hope.'"
JEREMIAH 29:11 (TLB)

In this book, as in my other books, I include quotes by such writers as E. Stanley Jones, Oswald Chambers, Rick Warren, Dietrich Bonhoeffer and others. Also included are several poems written by my beautiful life partner, Marta. She is now in heaven but very much with me in spirit in this ministry. Inevitably, this book will reveal me to be a "storyteller" with its many illustrations. Above all, this book is permeated from beginning to end with the Word of our Lord. I believe this gives it spiritual power and relevance. **Because Jesus is the Final Authority, I quote His Word on the male-female union many times in this book.**

Great spiritual revivals are happening in many parts of the Church in the world. Indeed, we need a heaven-sent revival in the Church in our land. We join with Habakkuk in his prayer in Habakkuk 3:2:

> *"O Lord, I have heard the report of thee,*
> *and thy work, O Lord, do I fear.*
> *In the midst of the years renew it;*
> *in the midst of the years make it known;*
> *in wrath remember mercy."*

Preface

In the midst of our diversity and in the midst of a fallen and sinful world, it seems inevitable that a "caring clash" would occur.

Some believe that caring for persons of homosexual orientation means affirming them, not least, as they express their human sexuality in same-sex, committed unions.

Others believe that there is another way of caring. It is to affirm them as God's creation, for whom He has a fulfilling plan without expressing their sexuality in same-sex unions.

Hopefully, we will avoid "uncaring judgementalism" and together seek for and recognize Jesus' Divine Design for the fulfillment of our sexuality.

Readers will note that this book is primarily about Jesus, His authority and teaching. It tells of His love for all of us sinners, heterosexual and homosexual. His caring is expressed in His reassuring words:

"I came that they may have life, and have it abundantly."
JOHN 10:10B

"The Spirit of the Lord is upon me,
because he has anointed me to preach good news to the poor.
He has sent me to proclaim release to the captives
and recovering of sight to the blind,
to set at liberty those who are oppressed,
to proclaim the acceptable year of the Lord."
LUKE 4:18,19

As we care about persons in different ways, may we agree that we shall not adopt the political agenda or cave in to the pressures of secular and humanistic power groups in the Church or outside? Jesus' Word and His Divine Design should be our agenda.

I hope that all readers will be clear on the meaning of the word, "homosexual". Some who are careless about connotations believe that a homosexual orientation is sinful. In this book, I try to make it abundantly clear that it is not the orientation that is the problem, but the sinful behavior and practice, whether homosexual or heterosexual. But to strengthen my consistent statements on this point, I quote from a sermon by Dr. Coleman Tyler, an Episcopal priest in Galilee Episcopal Church in Virginia Beach, Virginia, whom I also quote at the end of Chapter 2.

> "There is a world of difference between homosexual *practice*–and homosexual *inclination* or *orientation*. We **all** deal with inner inclinations or longings that take many different forms. And the truth is that some people have deep-rooted homosexual longings, and don't know what else to do with them, but to yield to those feelings, and live **out** what they feel **within**. And this is where we–the church–have failed miserably, to come alongside our brothers and sisters wrestling with these powerful feelings–and offer a safe place of love and acceptance–and the hope of restoration and transformation that Jesus Christ extends to all of us–homosexual or heterosexual. This Church–the Church around the world–needs to live our vision and *build better, stronger bridges of faith, hope, and love to* **all** in need–spiritually, emotionally, and sexually."

For those struggling with same-sex attraction, this distinction can be a tremendous gateway to freedom. It will lead to the realization that people are not created to be condemned because of their specific struggle. All people struggle in different areas of life, each with its own set of conflicts and consequences. Separating desire or temptation from action has been found to be a valuable first step in moving away from any addictive or compulsive behavior.

Inevitably, in any controversial issue, strong voices are heard, sometimes loud and negative, sometimes calm and thoughtful. Hopefully, there will be balance in our expressions of concern.

Each morning I sing the song, "This is the Day the Lord has Made". Indeed, I have something, not only to sing about, but to shout about. This reminds me of a statement made by the late E. Stanley Jones. He was speaking at a Christian Ashram (a Christian Retreat featuring reflection, repentance, resolution and silence for meditation). Dr. Jones was a flaming evangelist with a magnificent obsession for Jesus Christ, the Way, the Truth and the Life. At one point in his sermon I was so moved that I forgot who I was. I said **"Amen!"** loud and clear. Dr. Jones stopped in his message and said, "All my life I've been looking for a shouting Lutheran and at last I've found one!"

Because of the person of Jesus, all believers have something to shout about. With our voices we have the ability to speak words of freedom or bondage, hope or despair, danger or blessing. But it is important to maintain "balance" in our shouting. Here are some examples:

Shout danger:	This world is a mess. Look what this world is coming to.
Shout blessing:	This is my Father's world. Look who has come to redeem it.
Shout danger:	The Church has many enemies, within and without.
Shout blessing:	The Church has no rivals in the work of human redemption.
Shout danger:	The outlook for Church and society is dark.
Shout blessing:	The "uplook" is bright with hope.
Shout danger:	The way of the world is broad and enticing but leads downward.
Shout blessing:	The way of Jesus is narrow and leads upward to life.

These "Amen Blessings" are sounded in the midst of inevitable dangers in a fallen world. It is good to remember that dangers can magnify blessings even as light is magnified by darkness. Jesus spoke these words:

*"I am the light of the world;
he who follows me will not walk in darkness,
but will have the light of life."*
JOHN 8:12

*"In the world you have tribulation;
but be of good cheer, I have overcome the world."*
JOHN 16:33B

*"For the wages of sin is death,
but the free gift of God is eternal life in Christ Jesus our Lord."*
ROMANS 6:23

In times of darkness, tribulation and death, we have light, victory and life in Jesus!

A Personal Note
to Readers

This book has been in the making for over two years. These are tumultuous years in the history of our nation and of the world. It is a time of warfare–military, political and spiritual. It is also a time of change and crisis in the Church. Many movements in the Church seek to divide us. Only Jesus can define us and help us discover who we are. Only Jesus can bring us together as we have written in the preface, and indeed, all through this book. We recall the prayer of Jesus in John 17:21:

> *"that they may all be one;*
> *even as thou, Father, art in me, and I in thee,*
> *that they also may be in us,*
> *so that the world may believe that thou hast sent me."*

Other books that I have written point to Jesus as the way to an abundant life. They are:

Show Me the Way to Go Home–Journey to the Promised Land

A Strange Thing Happened To Me On The Way
*   To Retirement–I Never Arrived*

It's Okay Not To Be Okay–IF

Prayer in the Name of Jesus

Thanks to all the readers of these books and now this new book.
Inevitably, the message of this book is controversial for many, but hopefully not negatively confrontational.
In Ecclesiastes 12:12 we read these words:

> *". . .Of making many books there is no end." . . .*

At age 94, this may be the last book I shall write. However that may be and however our Lord leads, I am reassured that the first word of this book is JESUS and the last word of the message is JESUS.

"And there is salvation in no one else,
for there is no other name under heaven given among men
by which we must be saved."
ACTS 4:12

CHAPTER ONE

*"Jesus, God's beloved Son.
Listen to Him!"*
from MARK 9:7

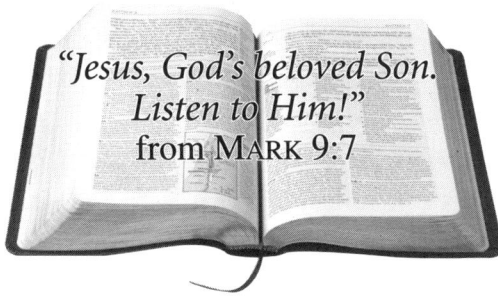

The Crisis of Christology

In the midst of present-day crises, we turn to Divine revelation as revealed in Jesus. Preachers, theologians, philosophers and psychologists are fallible. We do not depend upon them for ultimate truth. Jesus came, not only to reveal the truth that guards and guides us in the midst of a confused church and world, but also to be the Answer Himself. He is Incarnate Truth.

"And the word became flesh and dwelt among us, full of grace and truth; we have beheld his glory, glory as of the only Son from the Father."
JOHN 1:14

The Crisis of Christology

Webster's Dictionary defines "Christology" as "the theological interpretation of the person and work of Christ." Theology is "the study of the relation between God and the universe."

In 1678, John Bunyan wrote the world's "second best seller" (the Bible is number one) entitled, *Pilgrim's Progress*. Its main character is Christian, a refugee fleeing from the City of Destruction to seek refuge in the City of God. Today we are witnessing a "crisis flight in reverse", a flight of the human mind and imagination from God's citadel of eternal truth to confusion and error.

From the dictionary, we learn that the term "crisis" means "a decisive time or a critical situation whose outcome decides whether possible bad consequences will follow." To me the word "crisis" means something more. It indicates danger, but also opportunity and challenge. Crisis is the fulcrum of change, a decisive point at which a future direction begins.

It is important to view present-day crises in the context of the spiritual crisis confronting us today. Here is a partial roll call of present-day crises:

- Three million persons in the Sudan in Africa have been killed in wholesale massacres.
- The peace plan for Israel and Palestine is fragile. Middle East leaders are flawed in their rigid views and cannot lead toward peace. Terrorism stalks at their doors and ours.
- The Church is often giving an uncertain sound in its call for costly discipleship. The prevalent "gospel of cheap grace" is widely proclaimed.
- Military might is a popular watchword in our land. We suffer under the illusion that guns can protect us. Too many politicians can be bought by the National Rifle Association.
- Human greed is satisfied by wanton destruction of the environment.

•Millions of land mines litter the landscape of many nations, killing or crippling thousands of innocent children and adults.

•The epidemic of AIDS is a world crisis. Forty million persons are infected with the HIV virus. In 2002, three million persons died.

•We face a nuclear proliferation crisis.

•We face a human rights crisis.

•We face a hunger and malnutrition crisis.

•There is the crisis of political expediency in which the welfare of persons is expendable.

•Another crisis should be mentioned. I call it the Exploitation of America, especially children and youth, by the media, television and the Internet. Pornography and vulgarity are regularly featured. They weaken the moral fabric that has made this a great nation.

•A major crisis is the attempt to redefine marriage, neglecting the Divine Design.

•The crisis of authority, as revealed in this book, is yet another serious crisis.

•This leads us to the **Ten Commandments Crisis**. It is important to rethink not only the place of the Ten Commandments but also their application for church and state.

The Ten Commandments are more than God's law and prohibitions. They are His Divine protections for us. Instead of arguing about their place and use, we ought to build on the faith of our founding fathers and enshrine the Ten Commandments in our hearts.

However, questions persist in my mind, "Shall we delete from all historical documents any references to God? Should we remove from our currency and coins the inscription, 'In God We Trust'? Should we remove from any government buildings in Washington, DC all objects and pictures that reflect the faith of our founding fathers? Should we remove God, and thereby His love, from the laws that govern us?"

Jesus faced a crisis of law versus the knowledge and love of God. One of the Pharisees, a lawyer, asked Jesus a question to test Him:

> "'Teacher, which is the great commandment in the law?' And he said to him, 'You shall love the Lord your God with all your heart, and with all your soul, and with

3

all your mind. This is the great and first commandment.
And a second is like it. You shall love your neighbor as
yourself. On these two commandments depend all the
law and the prophets.'"

MATTHEW 22:36-40

So when we speak of loving God, our neighbor and ourselves, let us not forget the Divine Commandment to love.

As we face the dilemma of diversity in our land, we can learn a lesson from Mahatma Gandhi. E. Stanley Jones was a friend of Gandhi's and a partner with him in the struggle for the liberation of India from British rule.

In his book, *Mahatma Gandhi,* he tells of a conversation he had with Gandhi :

"How can we make Christianity. . .a part of the national life of India, and contributing its power to India's uplift? What would you, as one of the Hindu leaders of India, tell me, a Christian, to do in order to make this possible?"

"He responded with great clarity and directness: 'First, I would suggest that all of you Christians, missionaries and all, must begin to live more like Jesus Christ. Second, practice your religion without adulterating it or toning it down. Third, emphasize love, and make it your working force, for love is central in Christianity. Fourth, study the non-Christian religions more sympathetically to find the good that is within them, in order to have a more sympathetic approach to the people.'"

I recall this statement by E. Stanley Jones: "When India, a non-Christian nation, wanted to pay her highest compliment to her highest son, she searched for the highest term she knew and called Gandhi a Christ-like man."

At a Rotary meeting in which he was the speaker, he gave a magnificent address before a diverse audience of believers and non-believers, Christians and Jews, skeptics and others. He spoke on the verses from Ephesians 2:14 and 15:

"For he is our peace, who has made us both one,
and has broken down the dividing wall of hostility,
by abolishing in his flesh the law of commandments and ordinances,
that he might create in himself one new man in place of the two,
so making peace."

Following his message, he turned to the Jewish Rabbi sitting next to him and said, "Rabbi, was I too Christian for you?" The Rabbi replied, "No indeed. The more Christian you are the better you will treat us Jews and all other persons."

Thinking again of the Ten Commandments, should we not be grateful for the Divine reminder not to steal or commit adultery? Should we not be grateful for the commandment about bearing false witness against our neighbor, a reminder not to demean persons by contempt and exploitation? Should we not be grateful for the command not to murder, also remembering the words of Jesus that said, "To hate is to commit murder in one's heart"?

What do these thoughts on the Ten Commandments have to do with Jesus and the Crisis of Christology? The answer can be found in Matthew 5:17:

"Think not that I have come to abolish the law and the prophets;
I have come not to abolish them but to fulfill them."

Divine law is fulfilled in Divine love. Therefore, it would be difficult to think of the Ten Commandments and the law without thinking of Jesus, the fulfillment of the law. In Him the Ten Commandments can become the "Ten Freedoms" as we follow Him and His way.

St. Paul writes in Romans 8:2:

"For the law of the Spirit of life in Christ Jesus
has set me free from the law of sin and death."

In Matthew 19:16-22, Jesus illustrates a way to apply the commandments to our lives:

"And behold, one came up to him, saying, 'Teacher,

5

what good deed must I do, to have eternal life?' And he said to him, 'Why do you ask me about what is good? One there is who is good. If you would enter life, keep the commandments.' He said to him, 'Which?' And Jesus said, 'You shall not kill, You shall not commit adultery, You shall not steal, You shall not bear false witness, Honor your father and mother, and, You shall love your neighbor as yourself.' The young man said to him, 'All these I have observed; what do I still lack?' Jesus said to him, 'If you would be perfect, go, sell what you possess and give to the poor, and you will have treasure in heaven; and come, follow me.' When the young man heard this he went away sorrowful; for he had great possessions."

Jesus offered this sincere seeker eternal life. How? By keeping the commandments? There was something more. *"Sell what you possess and give to the poor, and you will have treasure in heaven."* But there was something more. *"Come, follow me."*

To observe the commandments is to follow Jesus and His way of love. To try to reduce them or to limit knowledge of them becomes an attempt to reduce the teachings of Jesus. He said in John 15:13,14:

"Greater love has no man than this,
that a man lay down his life for his friends.
You are my friends if you do what I command you."

Indeed, the Ten Commandments have much to do with the Crisis of Christology! In view of them, we find ourselves asking, "Who is this Christ and how do I know that His way is for me?"

The late Dr. Gordon C. Hunter, author, theologian and evangelist in the United Church of Canada, comments on this crisis in a pamphlet entitled, *Jesus Stands Alone*:

"We are confronted with a <u>Crisis of Christology</u>. But there is nothing new in this, for it is a persistent question in the New Testament. The Jews asked, 'Who are you?' (John 8:25);

the Pharisees asked, 'Who is this that speaks blasphemies?' (Luke 5:21); again, 'Who is this who forgives sins?' (Luke 7:49); the disciples asked, 'Who is this that even the winds and the waves obey him?' (Luke 8:25); Herod asked, 'Who is this I hear so much about?' (Luke 9:9); John the Baptist asked, 'Are you the one who is to come or should we look for another?' (Luke 7:19); Pilate asked, 'Are you King of the Jews?' (Luke 23:3); the chief priests asked, 'Are you the Son of God?' (Luke 22:70); and at the watershed of his ministry, Jesus himself raised the question, 'Whom do you say that I am?' (Matthew 16:15).

"All the while something else was happening. As they followed him around, it gradually dawned upon them that in Jesus they were looking into the face of God. So Peter blurted out, 'You are the Christ, the Son of the living God.' (Matthew 16:16); Thomas said, 'My Lord and my God.' (John 20:28); Peter again said, 'There is no other name. . .by which we must be saved.' (Acts 4:12); Paul states, 'He is the image of the invisible God. . .in him the whole fullness of deity dwells bodily.' (Colossians 1:15 and 2:9). William Barclay says that the most important verse in the New Testament is 'The word became flesh' (John 1:14). This statement has been called 'The Great Divide'.

"Of himself, Jesus said, 'God. . .gave HIS ONLY BELOVED SON,' (John 3:16); 'I am the bread of life,' (John 6:35); 'I am the light of the world,' (8:12); 'I am the way, the truth and the life,' (14:6); 'I am the resurrection and the life,' (11:25); 'I and the Father are one,' (10:30); 'He who has seen me has seen the Father.' (14:9). . .

"Most nice people today would not join with that crowd who shouted 'Crucify him.' But many might agree with those who said, 'Come down from the cross and we will believe on you.' And in doing that we are setting the terms of faith. We are putting Jesus in the witness box, thus making ourselves God. We make the conditions and require Jesus to fit in.

"Those who listened to Jesus said, 'He spoke with authority and not as the scribes.' (Matthew 7:29) That word 'authority' really means 'out of the nature of reality'. So to turn from Jesus is to turn from reality. To turn toward Jesus is to approach sanity."

> "...I am the way, and the truth, and the life;
> no one comes to the Father, but by me."
> JOHN 14:6

Now let me call the roll of other well-known writers. E. Stanley Jones, wrote in his book, *In Christ*:

"Other molds have proved too small. One by one they have been broken. Christ, the Teacher, the Greatest of all Teachers? Yes, but more, for a teacher imparts knowledge–He imparts Life. The Greatest of Characters, the Best of Men, the Highest Example? Yes, but more, for we are not to imitate Him in life, we are to receive Him as Life. Someone pinpointed in history, our Guide and Inspiration. Yes, and more, for we cannot live on a remembrance, we must live on a realization. A Martyr to the cause of the Kingdom of God? Yes, and more, for His death seems to have all the signs of a cosmic struggle with a cosmic result–the redemption of the race. Who then is He? He is the Word become flesh, God become man, the Eternal manifesting Himself in time, God simplified, God approachable, God lovable.

"In Jesus we have touched finality. We have seen what God is like and what life ought to be. The question is not, ' Is Jesus like God?' but 'Is God like Jesus?' The Bible says he is. We can think of nothing higher. We can be content with nothing less."

Dr. Conrad Bergendoff was a well-known Lutheran theologian, former college and seminary president, founder of the internship program in theological education, author and leader in the ecumenical movement. In 1937 he wrote a book entitled, *I Believe in the Church*. This book should be in the library and mind of every Christian minister and student of theology. In a chapter on "The Kingship of Christ", he gives us a theology of Christ as Lord and Saviour and a theology of the cross. Written sixty-seven years ago, it is urgently needed in the Church and world of our day. He writes:

"My first proposition is that the Church grows out of an acknowledgment of Christ as King and Lord. It seems almost a truism to say this. Yet current movements within the Church in America have so obscured this central fact that new emphasis is necessary. . . We have for so long deprecated dogmatic discussions about His Person that we have failed to realize that we have tended to settle the discussion by bowing Him out, not only from controversy, but out of temples as well. Some will say that the reason is a new conception of the meaning of the Bible. Others will find it in a shift of interest from theology to sociology. Still others will say that science has produced a changed mental outlook in our generation. I am not now discussing the causes. They are controvertible. The fact which I believe is incontrovertible is that the present generation does not take seriously, if indeed it even believes, that Jesus Christ is King. I am using the term in the sense of authority, an authority before which we humbly but devoutly bow and whose will controls our own. . .

"The regal gift which this King can dispense is the unique and all-important gift of the forgiveness of sins. I know how little impression such a statement makes upon a generation which feels its sins so lightly, and therefore sets so little value on their forgiveness. But in the darkness of mankind's iniquity the glory of the cross streams forth the more glorious to those who know the power of His grace. . .

"Because of the cross, Christ is King in the lives of His people. The kingdom is primarily composed of those who kneel, spiritually, before the Crucified One, and find themselves objects of His love Who is there exalted. On the rocky Acropolis stood the most beautiful structure raised by ancient skill–the Parthenon. But it was empty of any One commanding the worship of man. On the gaunt Golgotha stood a symbol of shame and death–the cross. But on it was

One who has drawn to Himself the attention of all mankind and the adoration of all who have come to know Him."

In his message, Dr. Bergendoff reminds us of the crisis of authority, another major crisis indeed.

Many years ago I was in Hawaii giving a series of messages at a Christian Ashram. Following the Sunday morning service at Prince of Peace Lutheran Church in Waikiki Beach, I stood with my life partner, Marta, waiting for a taxicab to take us to our dinner location. I went out into the busy street to hail a cab. Seeing one, I motioned for him to come to the curb. With eloquent gestures, I directed the driver who seemed reluctant to respond. With more vigorous motions, I finally got him to the curb where our group was waiting. Then I looked up. It was not a taxicab. It was a police car. This was the first time in my life that I ever gave orders to a police car. The policeman did not detain me but drove off with my apology.

There is a lesson here. How often we seek to direct God–to tell Him what to do. We seek to crowd Him into our small perceptions and finite minds. We want God to follow and bless our ways instead of allowing Him to direct our lives. Prayer is not self-assertion in which we seek to force our human will upon God. Prayer is *self-surrender* in which we open our lives to His control.

And so the ultimate crisis is the crisis inside of us. Will we choose self-surrender to the love of God and to His ways that protect and promote that highest love? Divine love has beckoned us all from the moment of our birth, and the varied crises of the world only serve to amplify the question. As we survey the pressing issues of our time, we can see a common theme, a shared origin from which these questions stem. C. S. Lewis, in his book, *The Problem of Pain*, says, "Pain is God's megaphone." The acknowledgment of the pain of this world, yes, and the pain inside of ourselves, will help bring us to the Healer, Jesus Christ.

So we ask, "What does all of this writing on the crisis of Christology have to do with the words in the title of the book, *Jesus–Final Authority on Marriage and Same-Sex Unions?*" Hopefully this question will be answered in the succeeding chapters. Any search for answers is in vain unless the Answer, Jesus Christ and His love control us. Hopefully, we will move from a "caring clash" to a "love one another as Jesus loves us" commitment. If we believe that the Church is truly the body of Christ, how can the Church's preoccupations be too far removed from Him?

In the midst of the present sordid, sexual revolution, we turn to Divine Revelation as revealed in Jesus. Preachers, theologians, philosophers and psychologists are fallible. We do not depend on them for ultimate truth.

Dr. Theodore E. Conrad, theologian, college and seminary professor and Bible scholar once said, "Never trust a theologian. Always check his words. You can trust Jesus!" He was not putting himself down. He is a theologian, remarkably gifted by His Lord with intellectual and spiritual insight. He was trying to make the point that if you want to find a word on any topic, a redemptive word of love, you must go to the Word made Flesh in Jesus. He alone is our Source, our Solace and our Answer.

So, from the Crisis of Christology, we turn to the life and teachings of Jesus, the Living Word and God's Final Authority.

CHAPTER TWO

> *"Jesus, God's beloved Son.
> Listen to Him!"*
> from MARK 9:7

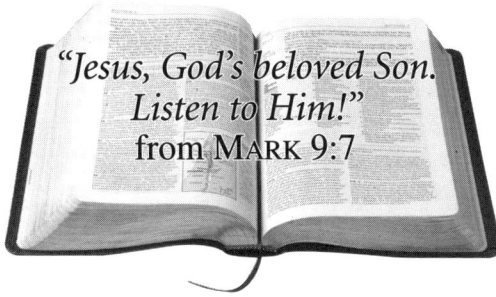

Jesus—Our Final Authority

In my reading of books and articles on the oft-quoted Biblical basis for same-sex unions, I have never found quoted the words of Jesus regarding His Divine Design for marriage. It is true that Jesus said nothing about homosexuality or same-sex unions. But in very clear words He gave us His Divine plan and pattern for marriage.

"Have you not read that he who made them from the beginning made them male and female, and said, 'For this reason a man shall leave his father and mother and be joined to his wife, and the two shall become one flesh'? So they are no longer two but one flesh. What therefore God has joined together, let not man put asunder."
MATTHEW 19:4-6

Jesus—Our Final Authority

I recall the story of a young theological student who was serving a congregation as a summer intern. One day, his landlady came to his study room with refreshments. Seeing the commentaries, sermon and illustration books spread on his desk and bed, she said softly, "Son, remember that there is some mighty good sermon material in the Bible."

Indeed, the Bible offers us protection against the barrage of human opinions, theories, slanted headlines and stories that come to us every day. We need the gift of skepticism that Marta Berg writes about in her poem, "Skepticism", from her book, *Seen and Unseen:*

"An acorn
fell on her head,
and Henny Penny ran around shouting,
'The sky is falling down.'

Each friend she met joined her
and the dread news became
FACT.

Around and around they went
until they met Foxy-Loxy.
He swallowed up the news
and the newsmakers.

Let me not ever join
a Henny-Penny parade.

Give me the gift of
skepticism

about all the words that are spoken,
and all the words that are written.

Let me test them
in the crucible of
common sense,
history's lessons,
and, above all,
Eternal Truth."

In Chapter One, we considered how crises magnify our need for God and His ways. We found that God's supreme law is a law of love. So we turn to God, His Word and to Jesus as Final Authority on marriage:

> *"Then the man said, 'This at last is bone of my bones and flesh of my flesh; she shall be called Woman, because she was taken out of Man.' Therefore a man leaves his father and his mother and cleaves to his wife, and they become one flesh."*
>
> GENESIS 2:23,24

It is significant that these are the final words of the creation story. In answer to the question of the Pharisees about divorce, Jesus said in Mark 10:6-9:

> *"But from the beginning of creation, 'God made them male and female.' ' For this reason a man shall leave his father and mother and be joined to his wife, and the two shall become one flesh.' So they are no longer two but one flesh. What therefore God has joined together, let not man put asunder."*

Again Jesus confirmed the Divine Design creation story as He spoke to the Pharisees in Matthew 19:4-6, repeating the same words:

> *"Have you not read that he who made them from the beginning made them male and female, and said, 'For*

this reason a man shall leave his father and mother and
be joined to his wife, and the two shall become one flesh'?
So they are no longer two but one flesh. What therefore
God has joined together, let not man put asunder."

In my reading of books and articles on the oft-quoted Biblical basis for same sex unions, I have never found quoted the words of Jesus regarding His Divine Design for marriage. It is true that Jesus said nothing about homosexuality or same-sex unions. But in very clear words He gave us His divine plan and pattern for marriage.

St. Paul also refers to marriage in Ephesians 5:31-33:

"For this reason a man shall leave his father and
mother and be joined to his wife, and the two shall
become one flesh. This mystery is a profound one, and I
am saying that it refers to Christ and the church; how-
ever, let each one of you love his wife as himself, and let
the wife see that she respects her husband."

Surely the words in Genesis 2, so clearly verified and confirmed by Jesus and St. Paul, should be words of Final Authority for us.

In the words of Jesus, we see a Divine Design for marriage. However, as fallen human beings, we continue to seek and to strive for life on our own terms, independent of God and His ways. At this point, we face the question, "If Jesus is not the Final Authority on marriage then who is?" Would it be the Church? Would it be our Evangelical Lutheran Church in America? Would it be the Task Force for ELCA Studies on Sexuality? Would it be the governments of Canada and the States of Vermont, Massachusetts, California and others?

If Jesus is Final Authority on the Divine Design for marriage, would He not be the Final Authority on same-sex unions, at least for the Church? Indeed, the Church should be heard and should speak out on the subject of human sexuality. The Church should also speak clearly on matters of injustice and discrimination against any group or class in our society. We need to be aware of the destruction of lives by the sins of hate, prejudice and lovelessness.

The Church should help protect vulnerable persons from violent words and acts, for in so doing we express the compassion of Jesus for all people.

There is another violence that must also concern the Church. The Church must guard against doing violence to the Word of God and to the teachings of Jesus. Rejecting the ways of God results in what is most violent to the human soul: separation from His presence and His best intentions for our lives. God's ways are established with us in mind and always point towards our highest good.

It is true that there can be many interpretations of the Bible and the words of our Lord. But is there any possibility of misunderstanding the clear words of Jesus regarding the male-female relationship in marriage?

If we reject this word we should not be surprised to hear some disturbing questions. For example, if we no longer believe that God has created all persons in His image, why is human life sacred? If we are the measure of all things, why not glorify sensuous rights and disdain divine rights? How do we know that it is wrong to kill? Because our Creator has written it in His commandments and in us. Why not condone human sacrifice? Why not permit a man to have six wives? Why not join in the popular "if it feels good, do it" campaigns of our day, and crusade for the human perversions described in Paul's letter to the Romans? Because this is God's world. He sets the standards. We are a people under God and under His cross in His world. The "God so loved the world" concept is basic in our search for morality, justice and freedom. Moreover, if we accept His John 3:16 love, we will recognize the worth and potential of every person created in the image of God. We will also love and respect ourselves.

In the ELCA Constitution, we have a clear statement of the foundation of our faith and practice. It is centered in Jesus. It is reassuring to read Article 2 of the ELCA Statement of Faith:

> "This Church confesses Jesus Christ as Lord and Savior and the Gospel as the power of God for the salvation of all who believe.
>
> "Jesus Christ is the Word of God incarnate, through

whom everything was made and through whose life, death, and resurrection God fashions a new creation.

"The proclamation of God's message to us as both Law and Gospel is the Word of God, revealing judgment and mercy through word and deed, beginning with the Word in creation, continuing in the history of Israel, and centering in all its fullness in the person and work of Jesus Christ.

"The canonical Scriptures of the Old and New Testaments are the written Word of God. Inspired by God's Spirit speaking through their authors, they record and announce God's revelation centering in Jesus Christ. Through them God's Spirit speaks to us to create and sustain Christian faith and fellowship for service in the world."

In 1969 I invited E. Stanley Jones to conduct an Evangelism Mission in my parish. He was with us for seven days, speaking to large audiences in the sanctuary. He also spoke in colleges and seminaries, to pastor's groups and on radio and television programs. I recall requesting that his first sermon be one that I had previously heard him give. The general theme was, "One Greater Than".

His scripture text was from Matthew 12:41,42:

> *"The men of Nineveh will arise at the judgment with this generation and condemn it; for they repented at the preaching of Jonah, and behold, something greater than Jonah is here. The queen of the South will arise at the judgment with this generation and condemn it; for she came from the ends of the earth to hear the wisdom of Solomon, and behold, something greater than Solomon is here."*

We quote from E. Stanley Jones' book, *The Way*:

"One greater than the Bible is here. We love the Bible, honor it, assimilate it, for it leads us to His feet. But the Bible is not the revelation of God. It is the inspired record of the revelation. The revelation was seen in the face of Jesus Christ.

18

Jesus said: 'You search the scriptures, imagining you possess eternal life in their pages–and they do testify to me–but you refuse to come to me for life.' (John 5:39, Moffatt.) 'Imagining you possess eternal life in their pages.' Eternal life is not in the pages; it is in Christ, who is uncovered through the pages. The Word was not made printer's ink. The Word was made flesh, not a page but a Person. . .

"Moreover, Christ was here before the New Testament. He created it; it did not create Him. It was His impact upon life that produced this literature. The Person is greater than the product. We love and honor the product, but only as it leads us to His feet and to an allegiance to Him. One greater than the Bible is here. . .

"One greater than rites and ceremonies is here. We do not disparage rites and ceremonies. They can and often do express our loyalty and love for Christ. They are the outer expression of an inner love. But to make any rite, any ceremony, essential to salvation is to make an idol of it. No rite, no ceremony, of any kind is essential to salvation. If it were, then we would be saved by a rite or ceremony. We are saved by Christ–not by a rite or ceremony. In front of Christ a rite or ceremony may be an idol and a stumbling block. Behind Christ, as an expression of our love to Him, it may be a beautiful sacrament. . .

"One greater than the cross is here. We sometimes say we are saved by the cross. Rather, we are saved by the Christ who died for us upon the cross. The cross can become a matter of contention instead of conversion if detached from Christ. On the cross He took into His own heart all we have done and been and made it His own. If therefore I identify myself by surrender to and faith in Christ, identify myself, not with my past life and its sins, but with Christ, who thus died for me on the cross, I am saved. But I am saved by Him, not by the cross. One greater than the cross is here.

"One greater than the Resurrection is here. We do not have

faith in His resurrection; we have faith in the resurrected Christ. He says, 'I am myself resurrection and life.' (John 11:25, Moffatt.) He is Himself the Resurrection. We do not have faith in an event, a resurrection, but in one who went through the event, and is bigger than the event. One greater than the Resurrection is here.

"One greater than the Church is here. The Church is a fellowship of believers, a fellowship around Christ, not around themselves. He, and not they, is the center. When they become the center, the light has turned to darkness. And how great is that darkness!"

Did you catch that key phrase from E. Stanley Jones, "The Person is greater than the product?" Just as this is true of Christ and the Scriptures, so it is true of us. Each one of us is worth more than the sum of what we produce in this life. As the only creatures made in the image of God, men and women possess a unique and intrinsic value. This is true for us in the Church. It is true for the homeless person on the street. It is true for heterosexuals and homosexuals alike. And it is on the basis of seeing one another as divine image bearers of One greater than ourselves that we can fulfill the call to love.

It would be difficult to find anyone more highly qualified than Jesus to be our Final Authority:

> *"And when Jesus finished these sayings,*
> *the crowds were astonished at his teaching,*
> *for he taught them as one who had authority,*
> *and not as their scribes."*
> MATTHEW 7:28,29

Through many words of Scripture and through many living forms, this Christ continues to reveal His truth to us with an authority and an authenticity that we cannot deny. Several years ago I met an artist from South Korea, Gwang Hyuk Rhee, who captured the meaning of the Word made Flesh. During the invasion of South Korea by communist North Korean troops, Rhee fled, seeking freedom and protection. He finally came to the United States. I visited with him in his home in

California. I think I shall never see a more impressive display of art than I saw in his home.

He had a vision of creating pictures of Jesus by using words and letters of the Bible. He also had the hand, heart and mind of a great artist. Over a period of two years, he wrote on a scroll, by hand, the 185,000 words of the New Testament. Led by the Holy Spirit, he was able to lighten and darken certain words and sections. This created the "miracle" of the beautiful face and figure of Jesus with out-stretched arms. He also was able to create the faces of 27 angels, each one looking at the face of Jesus. For me, this is one of the most beautiful pictures of Jesus that I have ever seen.

It is true that the world's greatest art is inspired by the greatest Person who ever lived on the earth. The Louvre in Paris and The State Hermitage Museum in St. Petersburg feature paintings of Jesus by the most famous artists of all time. It has been a memorable spiritual experience for me to visit these places. But it was far more impressive to be in Gwang Hyuk Rhee's studio in California. There I felt that I was standing in the midst of a miracle–the Word made Flesh. This Korean artist did not paint pictures on a canvas. Rather, he let the words of Divine revelation create the pictures.

In my visit to his studio, I saw other pictures. In a swirling picture of the cosmos, from creation to the last judgment, he brings out an unusual conception of Christ. He does this by writing by hand 100,000 letters in 1234 languages and dialects, using the words of scripture from St. John's gospel, chapter three and verse sixteen. *"For God so loved the world that he gave his only son, that whoever believes in him should not perish but have eternal life."* Thus we see the universal Christ revealed in the eternal Word, a Saviour for all times and for all nations. And we see Jesus as the King of Creation:

> *"In the beginning was the Word,*
> *and the Word was with God, and the Word was God.*
> *He was in the beginning with God;*
> *all things were made through him,*
> *and without him was not anything made that was made."*
> JOHN 1:1-3

Here we see the miracle of incarnation. We meet the person of Jesus in His word, and more. He steps out of the words to lead us safely through dangers and darkness to the Promised Land.

Isaiah presents some penetrating questions from the Lord:

> *"Who has directed the Spirit of the Lord,*
> *or, as his counselor has instructed him?*
> *Whom did he consult for his enlightenment,*
> *and who taught him the path of justice, and taught him knowledge,*
> *and showed him the way of understanding?"*
> ISAIAH 40:13,14

Surely, He who is our Beginning is also our Final Authority.

And what, specifically, is this Way of Jesus as it relates to love and human relationships, including marriage? To elaborate on the teachings of Jesus, I will quote from "The Church and Human Sexuality, a Lutheran Perspective". It was written in October of 1993 by members of of the Luther Seminary faculty to counter a position paper of the Evangelical Lutheran Church in America. It should be added that this is a statement of members of the faculty, but is not the official position of the seminary:

> "Jesus received sinners of all sorts into his company but did not thereby legitimatize behavior of all sorts. His acts of mercy were coupled with a call to repentance (Mark 2:15-17; Luke 5:30-32; cf John 8:11).
>
> "Jesus reaffirmed the integrity of marriage in light of God's intentions for women and men as revealed in Genesis 1 and 2: God created them male and female, and the two become one flesh (Matthew 19:4-5).
>
> "Jesus did not allow for greater latitude in sexual relations than is attested elsewhere in Scripture but, if anything, called for greater restraint. This is apparent in his stance toward divorce and remarriage when compared with Deuteronomy 24:1-4, and in the dignity he ascribed to celibacy (Matthew 19:3-12).
>
> "There is no reason to think that Jesus would condone

sexual relations outside a heterosexual monogamous marriage. The Bible contains no sayings of Jesus concerning homosexual relations, but neither does it contain sayings of Jesus about polygamy or incest, although these and other types of sexual relationships are treated in the Old Testament. We cannot argue from silence that Jesus accepted those relationships which he did not specifically condemn.

"Heterosexuals may find it natural to be sexually attracted to more than one person, and in some cultures it is possible for a man to establish committed relationships with two or more women; but the church has consistently opposed this pattern of marriage. Bisexual people are sexually attracted to people of both sexes and may find it natural to establish committed relationships with two or more persons, one from each sex; yet this too is unacceptable. Similarly, love and commitment do not legitimatize sexual relations between persons of the same sex.

"The report suggests that since people do not choose to be sexually attracted to persons of the same sex, but discover this to be their orientations, the attraction should be expressed in sexual activity within a committed relationship. Yet Lutherans understand that we are all subject to sinful inclinations that we have not freely chosen. Sin is a condition into which we are born. The specific sins Paul mentions (covetousness, malice, envy, etc., Romans 1:29) manifest inclinations we have not chosen, but whose effects we are obliged to control."

In the summer of 2003, in convention sessions held in Minneapolis, Minnesota, the Episcopal Church elected to the office of bishop a pastor who is living in a same-sex union. Following a broken marriage and divorce, he chose his present life style. This action by the Episcopal Church sparked a sharp controversy, not only among Episcopal Churches in the USA but also in churches in other countries. Church leaders in both western and non-western countries have condemned the 2003 assembly decision as incompatible with faith and practice according to the Word of God.

Now we need to listen to an Episcopal priest who, with many bishops and delegates in the convention assembly, was a strong "dissenter". I quote from a sermon by Dr. Coleman Tyler, given on August 17, 2003. The title of his sermon was, "A Tale of Two Trains". In his sermon he imagines two trains going in different directions in the Church:

> "Now the trains have not only been heading in different directions; they have been powered by different fuels. . .
>
> *Train A has been fueled by contemporary *culture*, personal *preference*, and human *experience*. (culture, preference, experience.)
>
> *Train B has been fueled by Holy *Scripture*, 3500 years of Judeo-Christian *tradition*, and Biblically-informed *reason*. (scripture, tradition, reason.)
>
> "Sadly, but with some sense of inevitability–2 weeks ago in Minneapolis, a tragic theological train wreck occurred–at the 74th General Convention of the Episcopal Church. After a couple of near misses over the years, the two trains of the Episcopal Church finally collided. . .
>
> *Train A, with **its** fuel, moving in one direction, and
>
> *Train B, with **its** fuel, moving in another direction.
>
> "And with incredible force–they collided. And the impact of this collision is now being felt and processed around the world. . .
>
> "Two trains; a tragic train-wreck. Now we must give it all to God, confident that nothing happens to His Church and His People that does not ultimately pass through the filter of His love. And so, we look to Jesus Christ, who sees the final **destination**–whose grace has brought us safe thus far, and whose grace will lead us home."

Jesus, Final Destination and Final Authority. Amen!

CHAPTER THREE

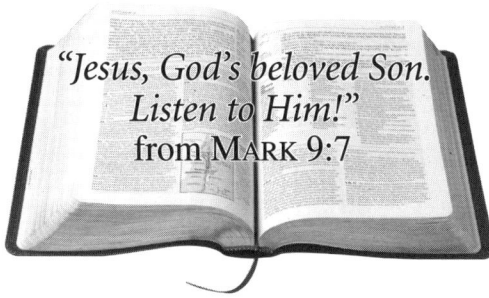

> *"Jesus, God's beloved Son.*
> *Listen to Him!"*
> *from MARK 9:7*

Jesus' Teaching on
Marriage and Divorce

What is Marriage? A better question would be, "What is marriage according to the Divine Plan of the Creator? If we want clear understanding of marriage, we should turn to the marriage service as outlined in the Evangelical Lutheran Church in America *Book of Worship*:

"The Lord God in His goodness created us male and female, and by the gift of marriage founded human community in a joy that begins now and is brought to perfection in the life to come."

"Husbands, love your wives, as Christ loved the church and gave himself up for her."
EPHESIANS 5:25

Jesus' Teaching on Marriage and Divorce

Fifth graders in a school were given a special assignment by their teacher. She said, "Draw a picture of what you want to be when you grow up." She received pictures of nurses, astronauts, teachers, doctors, candy store clerks, band leaders, engineers, big league baseball players and others. One little girl drew a picture of herself, shaking her finger at a map of the United States. She wrote, "President." But another little girl handed in a blank sheet. The teacher said, "Mary, don't you know what you want to be when you grow up?" Mary replied with tears, "Yes, teacher, I know. I want to be married and I don't know how to draw it."

How do you draw a picture of marriage? Only our Creator God can draw such a picture.

But many, both in secular society and in the Church, are drawing their own pictures of marriage. Their human pictures fade in the light of the Divine Design.

What is marriage? A better question would be, "What is marriage according to the Divine Plan of the Creator?" If we want a clear understanding of marriage, we should turn to the marriage service as outlined in the Evangelical Lutheran Church in America *Book of Worship:*

> "The Lord God in His goodness created us male and female, and by the gift of marriage founded human community in a joy that begins now and is brought to perfection in the life to come.
>
> "Because of sin, our age-old rebellion, the gladness of marriage can be overcast and the gift of the family become a burden.
>
> "But because God, who established marriage, continues still to bless it with His abundant and ever-present support, we can be sustained in our weariness and have our joy restored."

The Church has said it well but can anyone say it better than Jesus in Matthew 19:4-6?

"Have you not read that he who made them from the beginning made them male and female, and said, 'For this reason a man shall leave his father and mother and be joined to his wife, and the two shall become one flesh'? So they are no longer two but one flesh. What therefore God has joined together, let not man put asunder."

Here again we have Jesus' words on the male and female union. It is the Divine Design.

I recall a Re-imagining Conference which was held in Minnesota in 1993. Many Christian groups participated, including a delegation from my Evangelical Lutheran Church in America. The agenda and leadership were dominated by non-Christian leaders, some of whom showed contempt for Christian truth and doctrine. I believe that it was a low point in ecumenical relations and a massive cave-in to the enemies of the cross. The deity of Christ and the incarnation of God in Christ were repudiated in some messages at this conference. The term "re-imagining" can take the mind into unexplored areas for good purposes. It can also lead into forbidden and dangerous areas.

Is it possible that many leaders in government and in the Church are seeking to redefine and re-imagine marriage? This would indeed be a difficult assignment. It would involve redefining and re-imagining Jesus and His teaching.

I recall a startling thing that happened to me in a marriage service at which I was officiating. A few hours before the service I had broken my glasses. I thought to myself, "I know the service quite well by heart so I will be okay." But both in my conscious and subconscious mind I believe there was a lurking insecurity about not being able to read from the Book of Worship. I started out bravely, "Beloved in the Lord, marriage is a _____." My mind went blank on those two key words, "holy estate". At a time like this you cannot stop and say something like, "Marriage is, let's see, what is marriage?" You just have to find words and press on. So without missing a beat I said, "Marriage is a 'holy monument' instituted of God Himself for the preservation of the human family, and for the mutual help of those who enter into the sacred bond. . ." This was indeed a strange word to come to my mind at that moment of crisis.

The purpose of this illustration is to remind us that redefining marriage should not be caused by a memory block. We are to remember the true meaning and purpose of marriage according to Jesus and His Divine Design.

Walter Trobisch was a highly respected marriage counselor. For several years, he taught at Cameroun Christian College in Cameroun in West Africa. With voluminous correspondence and in many lecture tours, he taught the Christian concept of marriage in a setting of African taboos and practices.

Before his sudden death in 1979, he was recognized in this country and abroad as an authority on the Christian view of love, sex and marriage. Walter and his wife, Ingrid Hult Trobisch, have been very close friends to me and my family. We visited them in their home in Austria. There I read the manuscript of one of his books. I could not help but think that these two servants of the Lord were surely anointed to be brilliant writers and chosen of God to tell the world, and especially the Church, the true meaning of marriage.

I believe that Walter can help us in interpreting and understanding the words of Jesus on *leaving, cleaving,* and *one flesh.* He quotes the words of St. Paul in Ephesians 2:24 (these are also Jesus' words):

> *"Therefore a man leaves his father and his mother*
> *and cleaves to his wife, and they become one flesh."*

Walter comments on this passage in his book, *I Married You*:

> "This verse has three parts. It mentions three things which are essential to marriage: to leave, to cleave, to become one flesh."

Before continuing his exposition on this verse, Walter indicates that he was speaking in a time of moral confusion in Africa. Old traditions were no longer practiced. Age-old customs suddenly appeared out-of date. Tribes were broken up. Taboos were destroyed. They were facing confusing issues just as we are today.

"There can be no marriage without *leaving*. The word 'leaving' indicates that a public and legal act has to take place in order to have a marriage. . .

"Therefore a man leaves his father and his mother. Marriage concerns more than just the two persons who are getting married. Father and mother stand for the family, who are in turn a part of the community and of the state. Marriage is never a private affair. There is no marriage without a wedding. That is why weddings are often celebrated by a great feast. . .

"Real leaving and letting go–not only outwardly but also inwardly–is difficult for everyone. . .

"Read the book of Genesis and you will find the same kind of society. There it was a matter of course that women had to leave and become a member of her husband's clan. The unheard-of and revolutionary message was also that the man had to leave his family. . .

"It protects the women's rights. It aims for partnership between husband and wife. The message is, in other words: both have to leave, not only the wife but also the husband, and just as both have to leave so also must both cleave, not only the wife to the husband, but the husband to the wife, as our Bible verse expressly states."

The second part of Walter's explanation of this verse discusses *cleaving*. We quote:

"Leaving and cleaving belong together. One describes the public and legal aspect of marriage, the other more the personal aspect. They are intertwined. You cannot really cleave unless you have left. You cannot really leave unless you have decided to cleave.

"The literal sense of the Hebrew word for 'to cleave' is to stick to, or to be glued to a person. The husband and wife are glued together like two pieces of paper. If you try to separate two pieces of paper which are glued together, you tear them both. If you try to separate husband and wife who cleave together, both are hurt–and in case they have children, the children as well. . .

"Another consequence of this being glued together is that husband and wife are closest to each other, closer than to anything else and to anyone else in the world.

"Closer than anything else. It is more important than work or profession, cleaning or cooking, friends, visitors and guests. It is even more important than children.

"'To cleave' in this deep sense, 'being glued together', is, of course, only possible between two persons. Our Bible verse is an uncompromising attack on all polygamy. It states, 'Therefore a man. . .cleaves to *his wife*'.

"Cleaving means love, but love of a special kind. It is love which has made a decision and which is no longer a groping and seeking love. Love which cleaves is mature love, love which has decided to remain faithful–faithful to one person–and to share with this one person one's whole life."

Continuing his explanation of the Ephesians 2:24 passage, Walter comments on the *"one flesh"* aspect of marriage:

"This physical aspect is as essential for marriage as the legal and personal aspect. The physical union between husband and wife is as much within God's will for marriage as is the leaving of the parents and the cleaving to each other. . .

"Of course, to become 'one flesh' means much more than just the physical union. It means that two persons share everything they have, not only their bodies, not only their material possessions, but also their thinking and their feeling, their joy and their suffering, their hopes and their fears, their successes and their failures. To become 'one flesh' means that two persons become completely one with body, soul and spirit and yet they remain two different persons.'"

In summing up his thoughts on the teachings of Jesus and St. Paul on the leaving, cleaving and "one flesh" aspects of marriage, Walter writes:

"Where is the place of the child in our triangle (the leave, cleave, one flesh triangle)?. . . The place of the child is in the centre of the triangle. It begins in the union of the father and mother. It is surrounded by the love and faithfulness of both parents, and it is protected and sheltered by the legality of the marriage contract. This is the place of the child in the triangle of marriage. There alone is the atmosphere in which it can mature and be prepared for its own marriage later on."

In summary, Walter describes marriage that does not accept the Biblical view and the teaching of Jesus:

"If there is no leaving–(commitment, marriage) we have the *Stolen Marriage*.

"If there is no cleaving–(communication, love) we have the *Empty Marriage*.

"If a couple does not become one flesh–(cohabitation, sex) we have the *Hungry Marriage*."

Christ himself modeled the need for leaving as He left His father's house in heaven to come to earth as a man to seek, find and claim His bride, the Church. And so we have this model of the highest authority. In light of this Biblical "leave, cleave, one flesh" aspect of marriage, same-sex unions and marriages are revealed to be a departure from the Divine Design according to the words of Jesus:

> *"But from the beginning of creation, 'God made them male and female.' 'For this reason a man shall leave his father and mother and be joined to his wife, and the two shall become one flesh.' So they are no longer two but one flesh. What therefore God has joined together, let not man put asunder."*
> MARK 10:6-9

Departing from the Divine Design introduces real danger with tragic consequences. Let me illustrate the danger of redefining and re-imagining Jesus' teaching on marriage.

A pastor said to a lay person in his church, "Let's go to the racetrack."

31

Came the reply, "Why pastor, I didn't know you were a betting man." The pastor said, "Oh no, I don't go there to bet; I just love horses." Seated in the grandstand at the racetrack, they saw a very strange sight at the starting gate. A priest was there, and before each race, he blessed a certain horse. The blessed horse always won the race. This happened in twelve races. Leaving his place, the pastor explained to his friend, "I'm going to place a bet on the horse in the thirteenth race that I saw that man bless. Now don't think this is gambling or betting. This is a sure thing."

He placed a heavy bet on the blessed horse in the thirteenth race. The gates went up and the blessed horse bounded out and was far in front. He looked like a sure winner until he came around for the final stretch. There he stumbled and fell and died on the race track.

The pastor said, "I do not understand this. I don't know what's happening here. He was so upset and indignant that he went down to the track to confront the priest. "You blessed twelve horses in twelve races and they all won. You blessed a horse in the thirteenth race and I placed a heavy bet on him. He died, and I lost the bet." The priest replied, "My friend, you do not know the difference between a blessing and the last rites."

A question emerges from this story. Will the blessing of same-sex marriages be a pronouncement of last rites on moral and spiritual values upon which both church and state are founded? Does it mean the last rites on traditional Christian marriage as we know it? My answer to the second question is hopeful. Even though the concept of Christian marriage is under siege by the enemies of the Divine Design, Christian marriage will continue until the end of time. St. John the Divine envisions the end of time as a marriage feast (Revelation 19:7-9).

We need to be realistic about what is happening in the sexual revolution in our country. Many supporters of same-sex marriage will strongly deny that they are placing traditional marriage in jeopardy. But the gay activist movement and the homosexual agenda are indeed a threat to marriage and family life which, under God, are a cornerstone of society.

In a commentary entitled, "The Threat From Gay Marriage", which appeared in the *Boston Globe* on July 3, 2003, Jeff Jacoby writes:

"It is not by coincidence or on a whim, after all, that human societies since time immemorial have restricted marriage to opposite-sex unions.

"That restriction is part of a system of social taboos whose purpose is to protect families from the caustic power of unrestrained sexuality. Together with the ancient taboos against adultery and incest and the Western taboo against polygamy, the heterosexuality of marriage helps shield women and children from exploitation, cements the union between fathers and mothers, and bolsters the ethos of monogamy on which the dignity of marriage depends.

"Weakening those traditional norms boosts sexual freedom, but as sexual freedom rises, the stability of families and marriage declines. The slippery slope is real, as America's experience since the sexual revolution makes all too clear.

"We pay a price when we weaken common standards, especially those that pertain to marriage and sex. And the price of same-sex marriage. . .may be the ruin of traditional family life."

A decision by the Church to bless same-sex unions could indeed be the first step toward recognizing the marriage of same-sex couples as valid.

As we consider Christ's words on marriage, let us also consider His words on divorce. Where is Divine Love when it comes to the subject of divorce? We need to emphasize once again that the words of Jesus, which I presented as the Divine Design for marriage, were given in answer to the question about divorce. We quote from Matthew 19:3-6:

"And Pharisees came up to him and tested him by asking, 'Is it lawful to divorce one's wife for any cause?' He answered, 'Have you not read that he who made them from the beginning made them male and female', and

said, 'For this reason a man shall leave his father and mother and be joined to his wife, and the two shall become one flesh'? So they are no longer two but one flesh. What therefore God has joined together, let not man put asunder.'"

This is the word of our Lord on the subject of divorce. Divorce is the human way to deal with problems in marriage as opposed to the Divine way.

I believe that most persons would agree that divorce is not a good solution. There is too much brokenness, tragedy and suffering involved. Most persons would also agree that children are the primary victims of divorce. Here I would like to share a poem, "Beat of Drum", written by my life partner, Marta, in her book, *Seen and Unseen*:

"Rights.
It is a powerful word
in today's scene.

Drums beat
and banners float
to proclaim our rights.

Human rights.
Civil rights.
Rights of minorities.
Rights of women.

Rights, rights
and more rights.

But there is one
for whose rights
the drum seldom beats.

A small person,

vulnerable,
hurting,
pained as with the pain of raw flesh, pierced and probed,
torn, beaten, benumbed.

It is the child of divorce,
whose very birth
had signified
pledge and promise of
home and parents,

now denied."

If we could call the roll of divorced persons and their children, most would tell us of the huge price they paid in terms of struggle, suffering and pain.

It is important to note that Jesus' description of divorce as "not the way" became an indictment on the hardness of heart of the Pharisees of His day.

I have been an ordained pastor for over 65 years. In every congregation I have served, there have been divorced persons, many of them meaningful servants of the Lord and born again Christians.

In officiating at the marriage of divorced persons, I can recall only one couple that was reluctant to review the causes of their broken marriage.

Honest self-examination, painful though it may be, is necessary for healing and as preparation for a new beginning. A major cause of broken marriages is an immature understanding of Christian marriage. Also involved are the loss of mutual trust and the "lust for vindication" in which blame is attached to "him" or "her". For many thoughtful couples, these and other failures awaken a need for divine intervention, counsel and guidance. Prayer, penitence and new perceptions can bring hope for a new beginning. Thoughts of amazing grace and divine rescue can lead to a deeper commitment to their Lord and Saviour and to each other.

In some cases divorce is preferable to a continuing marriage in which lives are being destroyed by abuse, addictions, desertion, adultery and other problems beyond the control of the "innocent party".

Christian couples are aware of the serious problems they must overcome. They know that divorce does not come cheap.

Many years ago, we used archaic language in the marriage service. For example, we would ask the question, "Wilt thou take this woman to be thy lawful wedded wife?" In one service, the bridegroom was restless and perspiring. He replied, "I wilt." Many marriages wilt when one or both have refused to say, "I will" to the Creator of the holy marriage estate.

Present day statistics tell us that fifty percent of all marriages end in divorce and that sixty percent of second marriages also end in divorce. Broken marriages, broken families and lives, especially the lives of children, threaten the fabric of society. Strong and stable families are a foundation upon which freedom and democracy are built. What can we do about it? I am suggesting that we study and take seriously the words and plan of Jesus.

Both judgment and mercy are revealed in Jesus' teaching on marriage and divorce. We must not tone down His teaching. For many His is an unpopular word which they try to rationalize or misinterpret:

> *"It was also said, 'Whoever divorces his wife,*
> *let him give her a certificate of divorce.'*
> *But I say to you that every one who divorces his wife,*
> *except on the ground of unchastity, makes her an adulteress;*
> *and whoever marries a divorced woman commits adultery."*
> MATTHEW 5:31,32

St. Paul writes:

> *"Law came in, to increase the trespass;*
> *but where sin increased, grace abounded all the more."*
> ROMANS 5:20

Penitent sinners guilty of heterosexual or homosexual sins, adultery or unchastity, can be reassured by Jesus' love and grace which are greater than our sins.

One example of this reality can be found in the fourth chapter of St. John's Gospel. There we read the story of Jesus and the Samaritan woman. She came to draw water at a well. Jesus said to her in verses 13-15:

> "*Every one who drinks of this water will thirst again,*
> *but whoever drinks of the water*
> *that I shall give him will never thirst;*
> *the water that I shall give him will become in him*
> *a spring of water welling up to eternal life.'*
> *The woman said to him, 'Sir, give me this water,*
> *that I may not thirst, nor come here to draw.'*"

Then something happened which I believe led eventually to the conversion of the Samaritan woman, a sinner who had been married to five different men. In verse 16 we read:

> "*Jesus said to her, 'Go, call your husband, and come here.'*
> *The woman answered him, 'I have no husband.'*
> *Jesus said to her, 'You are right in saying, 'I have no husband';*
> *for you have had five husbands,*
> *and he whom you now have is not your husband;*
> *this you said truly.'*"

Then Jesus revealed himself to her as the Messiah and indeed as **her** Messiah. Instead of being a "divorcee", guilty of adultery and heading for inevitable pain and the tough consequences of her sin, she became such an eloquent witness to Jesus' love that a whole city came out to meet Jesus.

We are now confronted by what appears to be an inconsistency. Divorce and adultery are sin according to the Bible and the commandments. According to Jesus' teaching and His Divine Design, same-sex unions and marriages are also sin. How then is it possible for me to remarry any divorced persons and then refuse to bless and marry same-sex couples?

The answer lies in the teaching of Jesus on sin and grace, judgment and mercy, repentance and restoration. His redemptive love leads all of us sinners into new beginnings and into new life and hope.

However, those seeking the blessing of a same-sex union do so without the acknowledgment that homosexual behavior is identified in God's Word as sin. They deny that any repentance is needed because they perceive their behavior as "natural" and "right". This is what distinguishes the sanctioning of remarriage from the blessing of same-sex unions.

For all of us sinners, whether married or divorced, homosexual or heterosexual, there is a word of assurance and hope:

"For as by one man's disobedience many were made sinners,
so by one man's obedience many will be made righteous.
Law came in, to increase the trespass;
but where sin increased, grace abounded all the more, so that,
as sin reigned in death, grace also might reign through righteousness
to eternal life through Jesus Christ our Lord."
ROMANS 5:19-21

Amazing Grace, indeed!

CHAPTER FOUR

*"Jesus, God's beloved Son.
Listen to Him!"*
from MARK 9:7

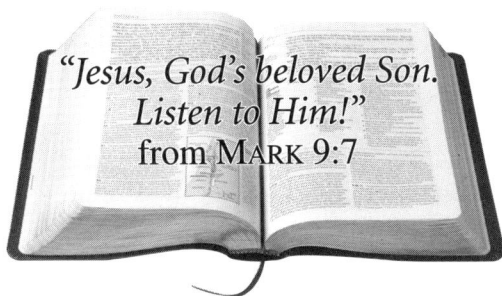

Jesus is the One Who Blesses—
Review of Misquotations

In addition to "What's a blessing?" let us ask, "Who does the blessing?" Do humans have the final word? Are we qualified to bless others? Shall we bless them? Or shall we accept the Divine Design and ask for grace to be worthy in Christ to receive the blessings He offers to us. For insight, let us look at some blessings given to us in Scripture.

"The Lord bless you and keep you;
The Lord make his face to shine upon you, and be gracious to you;
The Lord lift up his countenance upon you, and give you peace."
NUMBERS 6:24-26

Jesus is the One Who Blesses— Review of Misquotations

Let me begin with a story about blessings. A church member asked his pastor a rather strange question, "Pastor will you bless my Ferrari?" The startled pastor responded, "What's a Ferrari?" Came the reply, "It's my new car and I'd like to have you give it a blessing." The pastor became excited and said, "Oh, your Ferrari is a car. May I ride in it?" As they rode along, the pastor shouted, "This is wonderful. It's a great car. May I drive it?" As they drove along, the pastor kept shouting, "Ferrari, Ferrari! This is a great car!" Several times during the ride, the owner repeated his request, "Would you please give a blessing to my Ferrari?" The pastor stopped the car and said, "What's a blessing?"

Indeed, what is a blessing? The dictionary states that a "blessing" is "a statement of divine favor and approval; an invoking of divine favor. To bless means to set apart for holy purposes."

In scripture, God's design for marriage is made clear. In Genesis 2:18 we read:

> *"Then the Lord God said,*
> *'It is not good that the man should be alone.*
> *I will make him a helper fit for him.'"*

Following the description of the creation of the woman, we read in Genesis 2:24:

> *"Therefore a man leaves his father*
> *and his mother and cleaves to his wife,*
> *and they become one flesh."*

The Divine Word of Creation is made flesh in Jesus who is the Final Authority in every situation of our lives. We find these words written in Mark 10:6-9.

"But from the beginning of creation, 'God made them male and female.' 'For this reason a man shall leave his father and mother and be joined to his wife, and the two shall become one flesh.' So they are no longer two but one flesh. What therefore God has joined together, let not man put asunder."

When a marriage is blessed, two people are "set apart" for the holy work of becoming "one flesh", spiritually, physically and emotionally–just as God instituted it from the beginning. By definition, the word blessing has a divine connotation. This is especially true when it comes as a divine ordinance given to His people by the Creator.

In addition to "What's a blessing?" let us ask, "Who does the blessing?" Do humans have the final word? Are we qualified to bless others? Shall we bless them? Or shall we accept the Divine Design and ask for grace to be worthy in Christ to receive the blessings He offers to us. For insight, let us look at some blessings given to us in Scripture.

In Psalm 67:1,2 we read these words:

"May God be gracious to us and bless us and
make his face to shine upon us,
that thy way may be known upon earth,
thy saving power among all nations."

God blesses us to fulfill his divine purpose of making His way known. How? Through His disciples. Through Jesus. Through us. He has no other plan.

In Numbers 6:24-26 we have the Aaronic benediction:

"The Lord bless you and keep you;
The Lord make his face to shine upon you, and be gracious to you;
The Lord lift up his countenance upon you, and give you peace."

In the marriage service found in the *Book of Worship* of the Evangelical Lutheran Church in America, we find this beautiful prayer:

"Gracious Father, you bless the family and renew your people. Enrich husbands and wives, parents and children

more and more with your grace, that, strengthening and sup-
porting each other, they may serve those in need and be a
sign of the fulfillment of your perfect Kingdom, where, with
your Son Jesus Christ and the Holy Spirit, you live and reign,
one God through all ages of ages. Amen."

Indeed, an authentic blessing is essentially the favor, kindness
and goodness which God bestows on His people. Who then can
receive this blessing from God? The last thing that Jesus did before
leaving this earth for heaven was to bless His disciples:

> *"Then he led them out as far as Bethany,*
> *and lifting up his hands he blessed them.*
> *While he blessed them, he parted from them,*
> *and was carried up into heaven."*
> LUKE 24:50,51

They received His blessing. He loved them. He prayed for them:

> *"I have made known to them thy name,*
> *and I will make it known,*
> *that the love with which thou hast loved me*
> *may be in them, and I in them"*
> JOHN 17:26

And they were sinners. Simon Peter, a leader of the apostles, denied
with curses that he knew Jesus. James and John requested special seats
in heaven, thus creating dissension. All but one deserted Jesus and
fled at the time of His crucifixion. They were sinners like us. There
is hope for us sinners. Jesus blesses sinners.

How does this happen? How do sin and blessing relate to each
other? To answer this question, let us go all the way back to Genesis
3:15 where God, our Creator, speaks to Satan, the tempter:

> *"I will put enmity between you and the woman,*
> *and between your seed and her seed;*
> *he shall bruise your head, and you shall bruise his heel."*

Bible scholars differ on the interpretation of "the seed of the woman". Does it refer to mortal man and his struggle against Satan? I have always believed that the words of Genesis 3:15 give us the first announcement of the coming of the Messiah and His "it is finished" cry of victory from the cross. Thus we have the announcement of a future blessing in the midst of brokenness.

St. Paul writes about this in Romans 5:18,19:

> *"Then as one man's trespass led to condemnation for all men,*
> *so one man's act of righteousness*
> *leads to acquittal and life for all men.*
> *For as by one man's disobedience many were made sinners,*
> *so by one man's obedience many will be made righteous."*

St. Paul writes about the man to whom God reckons righteousness and whom He blesses:

> *"Blessed are those whose iniquities are forgiven,*
> *and whose sins are covered;*
> *blessed is the man against whom the Lord*
> *will not reckon his sin."*
> ROMANS 4:7,8

King David, a sinner guilty of adultery and murder, was blessed. But he, like the wayward disciples of Jesus, was a penitent sinner. Blessings from God are not cheap gifts. Where sin is not recognized, forgiveness is indeed a cheap commodity.

> *"When I declared not my sin, my body wasted away*
> *through my groaning all day long. . . .*
> *I said, 'I will confess my transgressions to the Lord';*
> *then thou didst forgive the guilt of my sin."*
> PSALM 32:3,5

Sin and grace, repentance and restoration, judgment and mercy, forgiveness and blessing surely are interrelated. There is a divine equation here that should remind us that we do not decide who is to be blessed. God and His Son, Jesus, to whom He has assigned judgment, do the blessing. And in the presence of God's holiness, true blessing can only exist where repentance and God's forgiveness have paved the way.

The Bible has many pictures of Jesus blessing repentant sinners. We read in Luke 7:37-39 that Jesus had been invited to the home of a Pharisee:

> *"And behold, a woman of the city, who was a sinner, when she learned that he was at table in the Pharisee's house, brought an alabaster flask of ointment, and standing behind him at his feet, weeping, she began to wet his feet with her tears, and wiped them with the hair of her head, and kissed his feet, and anointed them with the ointment. Now when the Pharisee who had invited him saw it, he said to himself, 'If this man were a prophet, he would have known who and what sort of woman this is who is touching him, for she is a sinner.'"*

Then Jesus told Simon a parable of the creditor who had two debtors. One owed a large sum and could not pay and was forgiven. The other owed a small sum and was also forgiven. Then Jesus asked Simon, *"Which of them will love him more?"* And Simon answered, *"The one, I suppose, to whom he forgave more."* Then Jesus reminded Simon that he gave him no water for His feet, but the woman had wet His feet with her tears. Jesus also reminded Simon that he had given no kiss to Him, but from the time she came in the woman had not ceased to kiss His feet. Then we quote these words of Jesus from Luke 7:47,48:

> *"'Therefore I tell you, her sins, which are many, are forgiven, for she loved much; but he who is forgiven little, loves little.'*
> *And he said to her, 'Your sins are forgiven.'"*

So forgiveness and blessing are interrelated. They are a picture of mercy and grace. Indeed, Jesus forgives and blesses sinners. But let us not forget the woman's tears. She was a penitent sinner. Jesus does not dispense "cheap grace".

Another picture of Jesus blessing a sinner is found in St. Luke's gospel, chapter 19. Many will recall the story of Zacchaeus who was the chief tax collector and therefore, in the eyes of the Scribes and Pharisees, a sinner. Having heard that a man named Jesus was passing through Jericho, he wanted to see Him. He was small in stature:

> *"So he ran on ahead and climbed up into a sycamore tree to see him, for he was to pass that way. And when Jesus came to the place, he looked up and said to him, 'Zacchaeus, make haste and come down; for I must stay at your house today.' So he made haste and came down, and received him joyfully. And when they saw it they all murmured, 'He has gone in to be the guest of a man who is a sinner.'"*
>
> LUKE 19:4-6

The story goes on to say that Zacchaeus promised that he would give half of his goods to the poor and that he would restore fourfold to anyone whom he had defrauded. Then we read the words of Jesus in verses 9 and 10:

> *"Today salvation has come to this house,*
> *since he also is a son of Abraham.*
> *For the Son of man came to seek and to save the lost."*

This is not a story of a man coming to see Jesus out of curiosity, or loneliness in the crowd or because he had heard that the man receives publicans and sinners. It is a story that tells the heart of the gospel, "God's search for the lost." It is the "God so loved story", the story of Jesus coming to seek and to save sinners. Jesus blessed Zacchaeus with a higher heritage and identity, describing him as "also a son of Abraham". Indeed, Jesus blesses sinners with His transforming love!

Jesus blesses sinners–sinners who trust Him to change them, and sinners who seek to make restitution for their sins.

Who does Jesus bless? We find the answer in the fifth chapter of Matthew in the Beatitudes. The blessed of Jesus are the poor in spirit, those who mourn, the meek, those who hunger and thirst for righteousness, the merciful, the pure in heart, the peacemakers, those who are persecuted for righteousness' sake, and those who are reviled and accused falsely. What do those who are blessed of Jesus receive? They receive the kingdom of heaven, comfort, satisfaction, mercy and a view of God. They are called children of God.

Lest we be carried away by all His blessings and by His promise of forgiveness of our sins, atoned for by His death on the cross, we are reminded of His gifts of accountability and responsibility. These are divine gifts that make us truly human. Our Creator does not treat us as automatons to be manipulated, or as puppets. In counting our many blessings, let us include the gift of freedom, freedom to choose. Our Creator does not use coercion to make us behave. We are free to choose good or evil, Jesus' way or our way.

A single, heterosexual person who remains celibate can lead an enormously fulfilled life, and persons of homosexual orientation, who choose to remain celibate, can also lead fulfilled lives.

Does Jesus give a personal blessing to a person of homosexual orientation who is attracted to a same-sex partner? Is there a blessing for heterosexual persons? Is there a blessing for all of us sinners?

Let us remember that we believe in the unconditional love and grace of God and not in "limited grace". At this point we need to study a word that many same-sex union adherents believe is simplistic and unrealistic. That word is sublimation. I quote E. Stanley Jones from his book *Abundant Living*:

> "*Both within the marriage relationships and outside them the sex urge can be sublimated.* This leaves an open door to those who are denied the ordinary outlets of sexual expression. The sex urge is the creative urge. But physical creation is not its only creative area. It can function as creation on other levels of life. It can become creative in the realm of the mind–creating new thoughts, new systems of thought, new mental attitudes both in ourselves and others. It can be creative in the realm of the social–it can give birth to new movements for social justice, for social betterment. It can be creative in the realm of the moral and spiritual–it can create

newborn lives, new hopes, new moral and spiritual movements.

"Some of the greatest work in the world is done by those who, when denied, voluntarily or otherwise, the normal outlets for sex, turn the tides of this strange power into creative activity in other ways. Their sex life is not suppressed, but expressed in other channels. Abstinence then can be healthy, provided the abstinence of sex on one level is practiced in order to loose it on another level. If sex is just dammed up with no outlet on any level, then it may prove a source of conflict and frustration."

Sublimation is an important concept, but there is another word, even more significant. It is "transformation" or "change". Many books have been written on the possibility and the impossibility of change in the homosexual orientation. Scientific minds and research specialists tell of dramatic changes in orientation. Others tell of the suffering and pain of those who have tried to change and failed.

However, the focus of this book is on Jesus, on what He has said and on what He can do. If St. Augustine, well-known Church leader in history, feeding on the lusts of the flesh for many years could be changed into a saint, and if sinners like us can be changed into beloved and redeemed sons and daughters of God, is it not possible that He can, by the power of His cross, bring hope and help to anyone struggling with his or her human sexuality? We can be sure that our Lord's tranforming power in our lives is an expression of his Divine Love.

Jesus said to a father who was pleading for help for his greatly impaired son:

> *"All things are possible to him who believes."*
> MARK 9:23B

St. Paul speaks of transformation in Romans 12:2:

> *"Do not be conformed to this world*
> *but be transformed by the renewal of your mind,*

that you may prove what is the will of God,
what is good and acceptable and perfect."

In the light of Jesus' Divine Design for the male-female union in marriage, how can we possibly say that Jesus would affirm and bless same-sex unions? Just saying that Jesus blesses same-sex unions and marriages does not make it true. As limited, fallible human beings, we can choose to accept or reject truth, but we cannot create it.

Review of Misquotations

We need to be careful about "saying who Jesus would bless". This reminds me of the story of one of the Lincoln-Douglas debates. Douglas was practicing his oratorical splendor with its power to "emotionalize" an audience. Lincoln, with his down-to-earth wisdom and his rational insights, at one point became so frustrated with Douglas's empty oratory that he interrupted him. He said, "How many legs does a cow have?" Douglas replied, "What in the world does that have to do with this debate?" Lincoln persisted and finally Douglas said in answer, "Four legs, of course." Then Lincoln asked, "Now, if we count the cow's tail as a leg, how many legs would the cow have?" Douglas replied impatiently, "Why five, of course." Lincoln said, "My friend you are wrong. Just saying the tail is a leg does not make it a leg!"

Recently I read a startling statement by a Bishop of the Episcopal Church. He wrote of Jesus' encounter with a Canaanite woman. We read this story in Matthew 15:21-28. The woman had come to beg Jesus to heal her daughter from demon possession. In verses 24-28 Jesus talks with this woman:

> *"I was sent only to the lost sheep of the house of Israel."*
> *But she came and knelt before him saying, 'Lord, help*
> *me.' And he answered, 'It is not fair to take the children's*
> *bread and throw it to the dogs.' She said, 'Yes, Lord, yet*
> *even the dogs eat the crumbs that fall from their masters'*
> *table.' Then Jesus answered her, 'O woman, great is your*

*faith! Be it done for you as you desire.' And her daugh-
ter was healed instantly."*

Commenting on this story, the Bishop wrote that the Canaanite woman's faith so arrested Jesus that He learned something new about God's mission for Him, which changed the whole direction of His ministry from an exclusive focus on "the lost sheep of the house of Israel" to anyone who was willing to listen.

Does this indicate that Jesus was not aware of His full and complete mission in this world? How easy it seems for many to reduce Jesus and to misinterpret Him!

In light of the fact that Jesus was "fully human", many may agree with the Bishop's interpretation. But He was also true God:

> *"In the beginning was the Word, and the Word was with God,
> and the Word was God. He was in the beginning with God;
> all things were made through him, and without him
> was not anything made that was made. . .
> And the Word became flesh and dwelt among us,
> full of grace and truth; we have beheld his glory,
> glory as of the only Son from the Father."*
> JOHN 1:1-3,14

In Chapter 9 of St. Luke's gospel, he tells of Moses and Elijah appearing with Jesus. What did they talk about? About Jesus' departure *"which he was to accomplish at Jerusalem".* One commentator says that this phrase is a "painfully literal translation of a Greek clause that could be rendered 'the fate that awaited Him.'"

Indeed, Jesus was aware of His mission and ministry in this world. It was directed toward "the least and the last", to persons hurting and scarred in body and spirit.

How does this picture of Jesus relate to same-sex unions? I believe that it is a reminder to us of the danger of misunderstanding Jesus' words and mission.

It is serious business to tone down the teaching of St. Paul on the subject of homosexual sinful behavior (Romans 1:26-27). It is more serious to bypass the teaching of Jesus on the male-female union.

How true it is that to change and tone down the truth as revealed in Jesus is easier for many than to change sinful ways!

It is impossible for me to think of Jesus as being unaware of the suffering, frustration, pain and temptations of persons of either homosexual or heterosexual orientation in the midst of their struggles with human sexuality. Is He not able to bring fulfillment in His way? Take a long look at the cross and see the price He paid to give life, and to give it abundantly to everyone who believes in Him and and receives Him:

> *"I came that they may have life,*
> *and have it abundantly."*
> JOHN 10:10B

Misquoting God is indeed a dangerous practice. Let us look at the history of Biblical misquotations. Where did they come from? This practice began at the dawn of recorded Biblical history. It was introduced by the devil, the father of lies. The first woman, Eve, told the destroyer of the command of God that they were not to eat of the fruit of the tree which was in the midst of the garden, neither touch it lest they die. Here is Satan's reply to Eve as found in Genesis 3:4B,5:

> *"You will not die.*
> *For God knows that when you eat of it your eyes will be opened,*
> *and you will be like God, knowing good and evil."*

Here is an example, not only of misquoting God but of correcting our Creator.

This misquotation, a fatal lie, resulted in disobedience to God's command, bringing sin into the human race and all creation. Great was the fall thereof!

In dramatic contrast, let us see what Jesus said when tempted to accept a misquotation of eternal truth.

When confronted by Satan in the desert, he had been fasting for forty days and forty nights. He was hungry. We read this story in Matthew 4:3-10:

> *"And the tempter came to him and said to him, "If you*
> *are the Son of God, command these stones to become loaves*

of bread." But he answered, "It is written, 'Man shall not live by bread alone, but by every word that proceeds from the mouth of God.'" Then the devil took him to the holy city, and set him on the pinnacle of the temple, and said to him, "If you are the Son of God, throw yourself down; for it is written, 'He will give his angels charge over you,' and 'On their hands they will bear you up, lest you strike your foot against a stone.'" Jesus said to him, "Again it is written, 'You shall not tempt the Lord your God.'" Again, the devil took him to a very high mountain, and showed him all the kingdoms of the world and the glory of them; and he said to him, "All these I will give you, if you will fall down and worship me." Then Jesus said to him, "Begone, Satan! for it is written, 'You shall worship the Lord your God and him only shall you serve.'"

The first temptation was to work a miracle for the satisfaction of a physical need. The second, to give a miraculous sign for personal recognition and gain. The third, to exercise political power.

Let us look briefly at the first temptation. Notice that Jesus said, *"Man does not live by bread alone."* Notice that key word, **"alone"**. We do live by bread. Jesus fed over 5,000 hungry persons with bread and fish. In Matthew 25:35, He said, *"I was hungry and you gave me food."* A famished traveler in a desert, upon finding treasure, cried, "Alas, only diamonds!" Indeed, we live by bread, but not by bread alone.

There is a lesson here as it relates to the claim made by some persons that Jesus approves of same-sex unions. Material hunger and human desire make it easy to rationalize, misquote or misrepresent God's word. In the January, 2002 issue of *Decision* magazine, Luder G. Whitlock, Jr. writes words we need to hear in an article entitled "Can't You Use the Bible to Justify Anything You Want?":

"The point is that the Bible was not intended to mean anything we may want it to mean. If we use the Bible to justify whatever we want, then we are manipulating it just as the devil tried to manipulate God's words. Furthermore, if the

Bible can mean anything we want it to mean, then the Bible essentially means nothing."

This reminds me of a custom which was used in churches in Sweden long ago. The sermons were very long in those days, so the sexton walked up and down the aisle with a long pole. When he saw someone asleep, he poked them with his pole. There was another version to this story. Perhaps it was adapted for use in an American church. The sexton would sit in the front pew with his long pole across his knees. This was better than parading up and down the aisle. The sexton kept looking back for nodding heads. When he saw one, he stood up, took his long pole and poked the pastor in the pulpit.

I am a pastor. I am called to preach the gospel, the full gospel. I need, if not a jab with a pole, the transforming touch of my Lord and Saviour. I also need the guidance, wisdom and anointing of the Holy Spirit to rightly discern the Word of Truth.

Did you know that Jesus was crucified on misquotations? In his book, *The Word Became Flesh,* E. Stanley Jones asked these questions:

"How far can evil go in a world of this kind? How far can force go? How far can lies and clever manipulation go? How far can you cover up the designs of evil in the cloak of good and religion? The answer is that evil can go a long, long way–it can put the Son of God, the Creator of creation, on a wooden cross–wood which He created. That's a long, long way. How far can force go? It can nail the Creator's hands upon the cross. And it can lift it up for all men to see what force can do. How far can lies and clever manipulation go? It can twist the truth of Him who was the Truth and make it into a falsehood and can thus crucify Him on misquotations. How far can evil designs be wrapped in the cloak of religion and good? It can go a long way–it can make evil seem good–they crucified Jesus in the name of God, His Father. They made it appear that they were protecting the sacred name of God. 'You have heard the blasphemy!' they cried. Evil, force, lies, perverted religion can go a long way in a world of this kind.

"They can do these things today and tomorrow, but the third day? No! For Jesus gathers all these questions in His body and answers them in His resurrected body and spirit the third day!"

Misquoting God and Jesus is a dangerous and devastating business. It means preaching salvation without a cross and salvation by human merit. It means preaching the false doctrine of universalism, meaning that God's love will save persons regardless of their acceptance or rejection of His offer of grace.

Misquoting God and Jesus produces humanism, rationalism, hedonism, agnosticism, institutionalism. These are often built on emotionalism. We need to hear again and again the clear words of Jesus regarding the Divine Design for the male and female relationship in marriage found in Matthew 19:4-6:

> "Have you not read that he who made them from the beginning made them male and female, and said, 'For this reason a man shall leave his father and mother and be joined to his wife, and the two shall become one flesh'? So they are no longer two but one flesh. What therefore God has joined together, let not man put asunder."

Without Jesus' word on His Divine Design, as churches and individuals we will continue adrift, tossed by changing times, opinion polls and secular agendas. We will always be seeking to justify or validate ourselves. All the while, He is saying to us, "I have come that you might have life and have it to the full." When we distort the words of Jesus, we distort His person. When we lose the person of Christ, we lose our source of life, and thus, our very selves.

We need to pray this prayer, "Open our eyes, open our hearts, open our minds." Jesus is the great opener of mind and spirit:

> "Then he opened their minds
> so they could understand the Scriptures."

LUKE 24:45

53

CHAPTER FIVE

*"Jesus, God's beloved Son.
Listen to Him!"*
from MARK 9:7

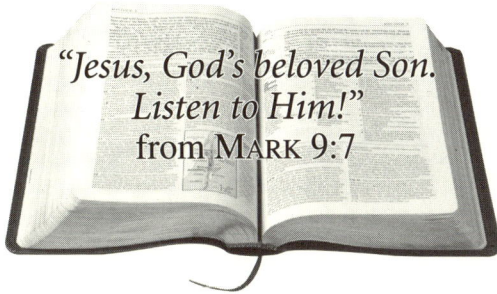

Jesus' Teaching on Sins of the Spirit and of the Flesh

What are we doing to get rid of sins of the spirit such as hypocrisy, injustice, conflicts, yes, and the trappings of religion? Will we surrender our pride and pretense for our Lord to destroy?

If we come to Him just as we are, with our sins of the spirit and flesh, then indeed, a miracle will happen to us.

"For God took the sinless Christ and poured into him our sins. Then, in exchange, he poured God's goodness into us!"
II CORINTHIANS 5:21(TLB)

Jesus' Teaching on Sins of the Spirit and of the Flesh

W e begin with a question that leads to self-examination for the author of this book. How can he possibly understand the suffering, rejection, and the battle for self-esteem of homosexual persons? It is easy to write what they should do and what they should not do. Can he identify with their needs? Where is his sense of compassion?

It is true that I do not understand. But I do know Someone who does understand. In fact, He has borne their suffering and struggles and burdens in His own body on the cross, and this Compassionate Saviour is the center of this book. What I can do, especially in this chapter, is to point out and warn against sins of the spirit, such as lovelessness, a judgmental attitude and substituting what is one's personal standard for the standards and teachings of Jesus. I can pray for the gift of openness, openness first to Jesus and His way of life for us, and then openness to others.

The question will persist in many minds, "Why deprive persons of what many say is a fulfilling life?" My reply would be that the love and compassion of Jesus is able to transform this "deprivation" into deliverance, into fulfilling lifestyles that only He can give.

Any sense of human deprivation that we may initially experience in choosing Christ and His way over our own natural desires quickly fades as we discover our truest selves and identity in Christ. The phrase, "deprivation and deliverance" raises another question: "Who needs to be delivered?" The answer, of course, is that all of us sinners, whether of heterosexual or homosexual orientation, need to be delivered. In other words, all persons guilty of sins of the flesh and sins of the spirit need to be delivered.

At this point, I believe that persons of heterosexual orientation need to face some troubling questions: Do we become so involved in judging homosexual sins that we are immune to the shallow and destructive view of marriage in modern society? Easy divorce, broken families and lives, severely scarred children and adultery do not commend heterosexual marriage. Why is the word "homosexual" for many synonymous with "sinner"? Why is homosexual orientation so often related to sinful behavior? Why do many persons of heterosexual orientation specialize in judgment rather than in empathy and compassion for those struggling with their human sexuality?

Hopefully, this chapter will remind us of the need for self-examination and for a "reality check" for all of us sinners.

We need to learn that both heterosexual and homosexual behavior that transgresses the Divine Design is sin and destructive for both individuals and society.

Our human sexuality is a wonderful gift of God. But to be obsessed with this gift is to lower our "identity quotient" and to cheapen our lives. St. Paul affirms the highest worth of our bodies with a very important reminder:

> *"Do you not know that your body is a temple*
> *of the Holy Spirit within you, which you have from God?*
> *You are not your own; you were bought with a price.*
> *So glorify God in your body."*
> I CORINTHIANS 6:19,20

A roll call of sins of the spirit includes moving from the witness stand to the judgment seat. As "usurper judges", we demean persons and label them as inferior. The true judgment seat is reserved for the righteous judge, the Divine Presence:

> *"For as the Father has life in himself,*
> *so he has granted the Son to have life in himself,*
> *and has given him authority to execute judgment,*
> *because he is the Son of man."*
> JOHN 5:26,27

Hypocrisy is another sin of the spirit. There can be no denying that some of the harshest words in the Bible are reserved for hypocrites.

Matthew devotes his entire twenty-third chapter to pronouncing woes and judgment on the Scribes and Pharisees for their hypocrisy.

Someone has said, "It is as difficult to get charity out of piety as it is to get reasonableness out of rationalism." The religious leaders of Jesus' day used piety as a front for their hypocrisy. Jesus said in Matthew 23:2-4:

> *"The scribes and the Pharisees sit on Moses' seat;*
> *so practice and observe whatever they tell you,*
> *but not what they do; for they preach, but do not practice.*
> *They bind heavy burdens, hard to bear,*
> *and lay them on men's shoulders;*
> *but they themselves will not move them with their finger."*

Such religion specializes in exploitation. Striving for self-exaltation, hypocrites treat other persons with contempt as inferior. If we treat persons, persons for whom Jesus died, in this way, our religious exercises become sounding brass and clanging cymbals.

Someone was boasting of being a "self-made" man. His friend replied, "Well, that certainly relieves the Lord of a great responsibility." Self-made persons love the wrong things. Jesus said in Matthew 23:6,7:

> *"and they love the place of honor at feasts*
> *and the best seats in the synagogues,*
> *and salutations in the market places,*
> *and being called rabbi by men."*

They love places but not persons. They love seats but not the Saviour. They love greetings but not God.

Scribes and Pharisees, hypocrites! Sins of the spirit! This picture is not complete until all of us sinners appear in the line-up. We are all sinners under divine judgment. But Jesus has a word of hope for us. We find it in John 5:24:

> *"Truly, truly, I say to you,*
> *he who hears my word and believes him*
> *who sent me, has eternal life;*
> *he does not come into judgment,*
> *but has passed from death to life."*

There is another sin of the spirit that is destroying both persons and nations today. It is the sin of hatred. Terrorist acts are destroying the hater and the hated ones in our day in many places. This sin of the spirit comes very close to home to many of us as we read the Word of Truth in I John 3:15:

"Any one who hates his brother is a murderer,
and you know that no murderer has eternal life abiding in him."

Another reference to hatred is found in Proverbs 26:24,26:

"He who hates, dissembles with his lips
and harbors deceit in his heart;. . .
though his hatred be covered with guile,
his wickedness will be exposed in the assembly."

Pride is another sin of the spirit. Its victim suffers from an illusion of superiority. In Luke 18, we read about a Pharisee at his place of worship, the worship of himself. He told God all the good things he was doing. He thanked the Lord that he was not like the sinful tax collector who prayed, *"God, be merciful to me a sinner!"* Then Jesus said in verse 14, *"I tell you, this man went down to his house justified rather than the other; for every one who exalts himself will be humbled, but he who humbles himself will be exalted."*

Stealing is a sin of the spirit, mind and hand. A helpful picture of stealing and theft is found in another poem by Marta Berg. It is also taken from her book of narrative verse, *Seen and Unseen*, and is called "Theft":

"There are those who steal silver and gold,
and there are those who steal
the most precious commodity of all–
the life of another.

Not with gun,
nor with ax,

but with words
and with scorn.

They diminish life bit by bit,
robbing another
of tranquillity
and joy
and dignity,
by complaining,
demeaning,
scolding
mocking,
nagging.

Their name, too, is 'Thief'."

I recall the story of members of a congregation who were very unhappy about a tavern just a block from their church. They felt it was contaminating their neighborhood. So they had a vigil of prayer. They prayed that the Lord would strike the tavern with lightning and burn it down. The tavern was destroyed by lightning. The owner heard that the members of the congregation had been praying for the destruction of his tavern, so he sued them in court. He accused them of being accomplices in destroying both his tavern and his living.

An attorney and the judge questioned the chairperson of the church board who was asked on the witness stand, "Did you pray that the tavern would be struck by lightning?" He admitted that this was true. Then he spoke these memorable words, "Yes, we prayed, but we surely did not expect this answer to our prayers. Therefore we are innocent."

The judge then said, "It seems to me that the only true believer among all of these litigants is the owner of the tavern!" Here we have not only the sin of the misuse of prayer, but also another sin. I call it the "lust for vindication".

We shall mention one more sin of the spirit. It is the sin of using prayer as a substitute for obedience. We can learn a lesson from a little girl who saw some traps to catch birds in a garden. She was distressed. Those birds were her friends. She said, "I have prayed that none of the birds would go near the traps." Then she added, "And I prayed that if any did, the traps would not work." After a long pause, and with a smile, she concluded, "And just a few minutes ago, I went out in the garden and kicked the traps to pieces."

What are we doing to get rid of sins of the spirit such as hypocrisy, injustice, conflicts, yes, and the trappings of religion? Will we surrender our pride and pretense for our Lord to destroy?

If we come to Him just as we are, with our sins of the spirit and flesh, then indeed, a miracle will happen to us. We read about it in II Corinthians 5:21 (TLB):

"For God took the sinless Christ and poured into him our sins. Then, in exchange, he poured God's goodness into us!"

Now we shall deal with sins of the flesh. Let us turn to the words of Jesus:

"You have heard that it was said, 'You shall not commit adultery.' But I say to you that everyone who looks at a woman lustfully has already committed adultery with her in his heart."
MATTHEW 5:27,28

And we read the words of St. Paul in Romans 1:24-27:

"Therefore God gave them up in the lusts of their hearts to impurity, to the dishonoring of their bodies among themselves, because they exchanged the truth about God for a lie and worshiped and served the creature rather than the Creator, who is blessed for ever! Amen. For this reason God gave them up to dishonorable passions. Their women exchanged natural relations for unnatural, and the men likewise gave up natural relations with women and were consumed with passion for one another, men committing shameless acts with men and receiving in their own persons the due penalty for their error."

We add here a brief comment on the sodomy law that was repealed by a recent decision of the Supreme Court. This decision prompted jubilation and celebration on one side and rage and dismay on another side. We shall not comment now on constitutional factors nor on the question of why heterosexual sinners should have an advantage over homosexual sinners.

However, we need the reminder that neither homosexual nor heterosexual sins should be approved. Sin against the commandments of God and against the Divine Design of Jesus poisons the mind, making intelligent thought and reason impossible. Sin cripples the emotions, making human feelings a dangerous guide. But there is a word of hope in Romans 6:23:

> *"For the wages of sin is death,*
> *but the free gift of God is eternal life*
> *in Christ Jesus our Lord."*
> ROMANS 6:23

One of the greatest tragedies to come out of this volatile and divisive human sexuality issue is for the Church to reject the words of Jesus and to agree with the states that are liberalizing their laws on marriage.

Dr. Theodore E. Conrad is a person of deep moral and intellectual discernment. He writes:

> "The recent published discussions of Sexuality seem to ignore or deny the fact that 'committed' homosexuals and heterosexuals need have any concerns about the matter of lust.
>
> "I ask: 'How can competent church people ignore the teaching of Jesus, so clearly stated in the Sermon on the Mount (Matthew 5:28)?' *'Everyone who looks at a woman lustfully has already committed adultery with her in his heart?'*
>
> "In the light of Jesus' statement, can it be imagined that He would approve of a woman looking lustfully at a man–or of a man looking lustfully at a man–or of a woman looking lustfully at a woman?
>
> "Two men may (and many do) become roommates and live lives committed to the good of one another and avoiding

lustful behavior. Two women may (and many do) become roommates and live lives committed to the good of one another and avoiding lustful behavior.

"One big problem of sexuality is always the potential for lust.

"Homosexuality, as such, is no sin any more than is hetero-sexuality. It's what one does as a homosexual or as a hetero-sexual which can be perverse–contrary to the will of the Creator–and therefore sin."

Sin defines who we are. Sin means separation from God, estrange-ment, a broken relationship. Sin is bondage to the old nature. Sin is a condition of the human heart, infected and polluted. Out of our sinful nature come specific acts of sin. We recognize our evil nature by the Word of our Lord and by our sinful deeds.

It is at the cross that we see the evil nature of sin at its worst. Sin, including yours and mine, nailed Jesus, the Son of God and Ruler of the universe, to a cross of torture and shame. But the picture gallery is not complete until our evil nature and acts are revealed!

Sin you say? Yes, for it is only as we understand the nature and real-ity of sin that we are ready for the life-giving and hope-restoring divine grace that is greater than our sin. In Galatians 5:19-21, we read of sins that prevent the sinner from inheriting the Kingdom of God:

"Now the works of the flesh are plain:
fornication, impurity, licentiousness, idolatry, sorcery,
enmity, strife, jealousy, anger, selfishness, dissension,
party spirit, envy, drunkenness, carousing, and the like.
I warn you, as I warned you before,
that those who do such things
shall not inherit the kingdom of God."

In the story from John 8:7-11 of the woman taken in adultery, note how Jesus exposed the shameful hypocrisy of the self-righteous Pharisees. They wanted to throw their physical and moral stones at her, claiming that Moses was on their side. Jesus said to them, *"Let him who is without sin among you be the first to throw a stone at her."* They all disappeared. Jesus said to the woman, *"Has no one con-*

demned you? Neither do I condemn you." Then He added, "*Go, and do not sin again.*" Indeed, adultery is sin.

Heterosexual sins are in epidemic proportions today. Call the sordid roll–violation of marriage vows, trial marriages, free sex outside of marriage, pornography, rape, incest, abuse of children and other deviant behavior. All sex perversions, whether of heterosexual or homosexual orientation, break God's moral law. They reject His plan of wholeness and fulfillment for His people. And more. These sins produce devastating diseases, sexually transmitted diseases, AIDS and others, reminding us that we cannot sin and avoid the consequences. Sin violates human dignity. Moreover, sex sins poison and weaken the social order. They destroy the very foundations of society such as the home and family life. Sex sins, and indeed all sins, are self-destructive. They are against life. Evil is "live" spelled backwards.

There are also homosexual sins. Here we deal, not with homosexual orientation, but with homosexual behavior and practice.

Paul gives a vivid picture of homosexual perversions in Romans 1:26B,27A:

> "*Their women exchanged natural relations for unnatural,*
> *and the men likewise gave up natural relations with women*
> *and were consumed with passion for one another.*"

Charles Colson, founder of Prison Fellowship, in an editorial in *Christianity Today* (October, 2003), has a significant statement on marriage:

> "Clearly, our culture has severed the tie between marriage and its purposes: procreation and spousal unity. Even many Christians accept the notion that sex is intended primarily for pleasure. And if sex is merely recreational, what's the rationale for denying marriage to gay couples? If heterosexuals can legalize *their* "recreation", why shouldn't gays?
>
> "Christians have to regain the high moral ground, making–to our secular neighbors–the natural order arguments that define the purposes of sex as unitive and procreative, and marriage as the stable, one-man, one-woman institution

in which to rear children. This means we will have to be just as critical of heterosexuals engaging in extramarital, recreational sex as we are of homosexual behavior."

Let us thank God that He will not let us sin undisturbed. This is true whether it be in the sins described in the first chapter of Romans, in the sensuous sins of King David, in the sins of pride and pretense or in your sins and mine. The question we should be facing is not how we can continue in sin, but rather, how to get rid of sin. In Psalm 49:8 (TLB) we read how not to get rid of sin:

*"For a soul is far too precious to be ransomed
by mere earthly wealth."*

Likewise, a person is far too precious to be ransomed by twenty-first century indulgences dispensed by purveyors of cheap grace.

How do unrepentant persons try to get rid of sin? They try to mythologize it, to legalize it and to institutionalize it. Some commercialize it and some demonize it (the devil made me do it). Others try to camouflage sin. Sin is a harsh and unpopular word. Pornography is called art, lying is called propaganda and obscenity is called freedom of speech. License comes across as liberty and lust as love. Abortion is called "the right to choose" and prejudice is camouflaged as individual rights.

In reading this chapter, it may appear to some that there is more emphasis on sin than on grace. Too much talk about sin will turn many away from the church and the gospel. But for me, to mention sin is to magnify grace. Grace is for sinners only:

*"But God shows his love for us in that
while we were yet sinners Christ died for us."*
ROMANS 5:8

Let us accept the teachings of Jesus and be led by the winds of the Holy Spirit rather than by the winds of secularism and emotionalism. What did Jesus say? Let us hear it again:

"Have you not read that he who made them from the

beginning made them male and female, and said, 'For this reason a man shall leave his father and mother and be joined to his wife, and the two shall become one flesh'? So they are no longer two but one flesh. What therefore God has joined together, let not man put asunder."

MATTHEW 19:4-6

Let us receive these words as the design of a loving Saviour, trusting in His abundant grace to cover all our sins, sins of the spirit and sins of the flesh.

CHAPTER 6

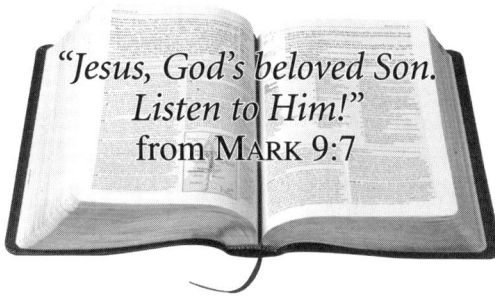

"Jesus, God's beloved Son.
Listen to Him!"
from MARK 9:7

Jesus and His
Calvary Love

It was the worst of all times on a hill outside the Holy City. There the very people
Jesus loved and came to rescue and save, spit
in his face, held him in derision and nailed
him to a cross of agony and torment. It was
earth's darkest hour.

It was the worst of times for the disciples
and followers of Jesus when their Lord was
killed. Their hopes died with Him. But it
was the best of times on that first Easter
morning when the tomb was empty and Jesus
came out alive to be with them forever.

"But the angel said to the women, 'Do not be afraid;
for I know that you seek Jesus who was crucified.
He is not here; for he has risen, as he said.
Come, see the place where he lay.'"
MATTHEW 28:5,6

Jesus and His Calvary Love

In my 67 years of ordained ministry, I have officiated at many marriage services. Years ago in the liturgy of the Augustana Lutheran Church, the marriage service began with these words: "Marriage is a holy estate instituted of God himself for the preservation of the human family, and for the mutual help of those who enter into this sacred bond, to lighten the burdens of life, to alleviate its unavoidable cares, and by careful nurture to provide for the happiness of posterity. This is a holy institution; its obligations and objects are likewise holy."

Today in the *Book of Worship* of the Evangelical Lutheran Church in America, we find these words in the marriage service: "The Lord God who created our first parents and established them in marriage, establish and sustain you, that you may find delight in each other and grow in holy love until your life's end."

I have had the joy of participating in some very special celebrations of marriage with my three children and three of my grandchildren. To dramatize marital love and divine love, I invite readers to look in on the marriage of my grandson, Jeff, and his bride, Moni. It took place in the Augustana Lutheran Church in Minneapolis, Minnesota. This service and the message of the cross lifted up across the world will remind us of the title of this chapter.

In my marriage homily I shared with them a message in living color. My text was found in the three magnificent stained glass windows in the sanctuary–the Calvary window, the Good Shepherd window and the Ascension window. The theme of my homily was "Caring Arms".

I asked Jeff and Moni to look at the Calvary window, there to see their Lord and Saviour dying for them on a cross. "How much does He love **you**? How greatly does He care for **you**? His caring arms, outstretched on that cross, give the answer. It's right there in living color from the window and it's in God's Holy Book".

I quote from the homily:

"His outstretched arms define who you really are. You are more than lovers, you are more than husband and wife, you are more than vulnerable and very human persons, you are more than lapsing lovers who sometimes will fail each other. His loving and caring arms remind you that you are redeemed sinners, cleansed, loved by God, precious in His sight. There you see arms that will always remind you of the love that will never let go of you."

The sight of those caring arms reflects the true meaning of love. Jesus said:

"This is my commandment,
that you love one another as I have loved you."
JOHN 15:12

I reminded Jeff and Moni that they need more than human love. They need the love for each other that Jesus puts into their hearts. I also reminded them that very often their arms would enfold each other in a fond embrace. Also, that someday their arms would hold beautiful babies. And more. If they understood the Calvary arms, their arms would be extended far beyond themselves. I quote again from the homily:

"We have talked about caring arms, Divine arms. Now let me talk again about your arms. If you believe the message of the window, then your arms will surely be caring arms for others. From this altar you are going into a tough world filled with lost, confused and hurting persons. God is bringing you together so that your arms of love will unfold to lift and bless persons in need. Your arms will help rescue them, feed them and set them free from bondage. God wants to use your arms for human rights causes, for ministries of compassion, for seeking to right the devastating wrongs in society. And it is my prayer, Jeff and Moni, that you will never get so caught up in these great causes that you will lose sight of our Lord's caring arms for them and for you."

In a pre-marriage counseling session, I shared two stories with Jeff and Moni. In the first story, the bridegroom asked the pastor, "How much do I owe you?" The pastor replied, "Whatever you think it's worth." The young man reached into his pocket, took out a dollar bill and handed it to the pastor. Then the pastor gave him fifty cents in change. Neither of them thought the marriage was of much worth.

I reminded Jeff and Moni that theirs was a very costly marriage. In fact, it was priceless in terms of the gift of family and friends, the gift of each other and, above all, the price the Lord paid to cleanse them and make them worthy of each other.

The second story I shared with them was about a bride and bridegroom at the altar. During the service, the bride was indeed beautiful, calm and poised, but the bridegroom was very nervous. He fidgeted and moved his hands in and out of his pockets. The best man whispered, "John, what happened? Did you lose the ring?" John replied, "Worse than that. I've lost my enthusiasm!"

The word "enthusiasm" comes from the Greek "en" and "theos"–"in God". This is indeed a mystery described in the Bible in this way:

"To them God chose to make known
how great among the Gentiles are the riches of the glory
of this mystery, which is Christ in you, the hope of glory."
COLOSSIANS 1:27

"When anyone is united to Christ, there is a new world;
the old order has gone, and a new order has already begun."
2 CORINTHIANS 5:17 (NEB)

Now I invite you to come with me on a tour of the cross. Perhaps many travelers would not see what I saw. Hopefully this tour will remind many of the cross on which Jesus died. This is indeed a picture of redeeming love.

In two visits to Russia before the Iron Curtain came down, I saw the cross. An oppressive communist government tried to get rid of all dissident persons and more. They tried to get rid of all vestiges of Christianity. But in this hostile environment I saw the cross on top of the high steeples of magnificent cathedrals. The cross is the symbol of the most costly love of all–God's selfless love for humanity that caused Him to give His own life.

In a visit to the Taj Mahal in India, I saw the cross. It was indeed a strange place to see a cross. This world famous monument, a magnificent architectural accomplishment and one of the seven wonders of the world, was built to memorialize Mumtaz Mahal, a compassionate empress, by her husband, Shah Jeban, emperor of India. From the top of the tower there was a long golden rod at the end of which was a burning candle over the tomb of the empress. As I looked up I saw a horizontal rod. There I saw the cross. I am sure that the architect and many others saw only the wonder and glory of a person. All I know is that on that day I saw the cross.

I recall that on two visits to Seoul, South Korea I saw the greatest panorama of church spires I have ever seen. There were hundreds of them, rising heavenward, each with a cross on the top.

In Hiroshima, Japan, I saw the cross. I was at a memorial service with the pastor of a church that had been destroyed by our atomic bomb. Many church members had perished, but out of the ashes and the devastation had risen a beautiful new church building under the cross. It was one of the most moving moments of my life when I was asked to speak and pray at that memorial gathering. But I could tell of the power of the cross in the lives of those who perished and the lives of us who were gathered there. I prayed, "God have mercy on the tens of thousands still dying slowly and tortuously as victims of the bomb. Lord have mercy upon Japan. Lord have mercy upon the United States of America. Lord have mercy on your Church. And Lord, may this never happen again as we follow your way, the way of the Cross."

On the front page of the Minneapolis *Star Tribune*, September 10, 2003, I saw an unusual picture of a cross. It was formed by steel beams and stood over the temporary memorial at the Trade Center in New York. The picture was part of a story, entitled, "Remember 9/11, a City Scarred but on the Rise." No mention was made of the cross and its meaning. But the picture was worth countless words. For me, it meant new life and hope rising from the ruins. Acts of heroism, sacrifice and self-giving abound in the 9/11 story. Again we quote the word of the cross as found in John 15:13:

> *"Greater love has no man than this,*
> *that a man lay down his life for his friends."*

Our tour of the cross leads us next to the bedside of a woman named Cindy. I received a call from her mother saying that Cindy was critically ill. I remembered her. Ten years before she had been active in the Crossroad program of Augustana Lutheran Church. With my associate pastor, Kay Jurgenson, we hurried to the hospital. Cindy, now 22 years old, was dying. On the table beside her bed was a picture of her taken ten years earlier. She and I were on the cover of "The Lutheran" magazine. The lead story was about Native Americans, African Americans and others participating in the Crossroad program of Augustana Lutheran Church. We reminded Cindy of those great days when she had heard of God's love for her, and of Jesus who was still with her.

I looked at Cindy's mother who, with many brothers and sisters, was in the room. She opened her hand to reveal a cross that I had given to her many years before. We prayed. We shared. Then Pastor Kay removed the beautiful gold cross from around her neck and placed it on Cindy. She died under the cross. Jesus' love never let go of that beautiful twelve-year old girl. The way of the cross leads Home. Cindy had not been in church for many years but she could not die without hearing once more of the message and hope of the cross.

We need to hear more about Jesus and His Calvary love and the way of the cross. When we talk about the cross, we inevitably face the reality of sin. This is neither a palatable or popular subject in our day. Salvation is offered to many without the message of the cross and of the risen Saviour.

Someone said, "A denatured gospel can never capture and convert a depraved humanity." A long and reverent look at the cross could be the cure for shallow concepts of love.

In his book, *Christ's Alternative to Communism*, E. Stanley Jones has a significant statement on the cross:

> "Then came the supreme attempt to block him (Jesus) and his Kingdom when the nation combined to stop him by a cross. Christ and Evil met face to face that day. There stood before him and his Kingdom incarnate Evil: the Pharisee–proud, hard outwardism; the Sadducee–shrewd materialism; the Chief Priests–vested interests; the Herodians–political sycophancy; the scribes–letter-worship of the past; Pontius Pilate–imperialism demanding supreme allegiance: the People–apathy against change; the Soldiers–militarism, hard and unrelenting. They all combined to stop him and his subversive Kingdom. But even on a cross he was master of the situation: he opened the gates of paradise to a dying thief, dispensed forgiveness to his murderers, made provision for his mother's sustenance, and showed such regnancy that the officer in charge of the tragedy smote his breast and said that he was the Son of God. God and the officer agreed, and the sign of that agreement is an Easter morning. Stop him by a cross? He used that very cross to redeem a world.

He adds in his book, *A Song of Ascents*:

> "When Jesus cried on the cross, 'It is finished,' it was not a cry of termination–'My course is finished, my life is over, I am finished'; it was a cry not of termination, but of triumph–'It,' the purpose for which I came, 'is finished.' That purpose was redemption; that purpose is fulfilled: 'I have redeemed a race. It is now for them to accept it, individually and collectively. I cannot force it upon them, for forced goodness is not goodness'...So he must wait patiently till the self-inflicted sufferings, brought on by man's self-will and waywardness, drive him to his Sufferings, for relief and release."

In his book, *My Utmost For His Highest*, Oswald Chambers wrote:

> "The bedrock of our Christian faith is the unmerited, fath-
> omless marvel of the love of God exhibited on the Cross of
> Calvary, a love we never can and never shall merit. Paul says
> this is the reason we are more than conquerors in all these
> things, super-victors, with a joy we would not have but for the
> very things which look as if they are going to overwhelm us. . .
>
> "We are more than conquerors through Him *in* all these
> things, not in spite of them, but in the midst of them."

The story of Jesus and His Calvary love runs like a red thread, like
a crimson tide of redemptive love, from the book of Genesis to the
last book of the Bible, the Revelation of Saint John.

In Genesis 3:15, it was the worst of times when our first parents
were to be banished from the Garden of Eden, and the ploughshare
drawn over paradise. We cannot sin against a holy God and get by.
But it was also the best of times in terms of the divine announcement. God spoke to the tempter, Satan, saying:

> *"I will put enmity between you and the woman,*
> *and between your seed and her seed;*
> *he shall bruise your head, and you shall bruise his heel."*

It was the worst of times when flood waters covered the earth, and
all living souls perished, except for eight persons, the family of Noah.
But it was the best of times as we see a huge boat riding the crest, a
place of refuge from death. (Genesis 7:21-23.) It was the worst of times
when the angel of death stalked the land of Egypt, killing the firstborn
in every Egyptian home. There was wailing and weeping. But it was
the best of times as we see blood on the doorposts of the Israelite
homes, and everyone safe on the inside. (Exodus 12:21-23.) It was the
worst of times when the rebellious Israelites were dying on every hand,
bitten by poisonous snakes. But lift up your eyes. It was also the best of
times. There was a bronze serpent on a pole. Each person who looked
at it was healed. (Numbers 21:7-9.) It was the worst of times some
two thousand years ago when Israel was under the cruel oppression

of the Roman government, and under the ruthless tyranny of a king like Herod. We hear the cry of a newborn baby in a manger in Bethlehem. It was also the best of times. Unto you is born a Saviour!

"And the angel said to them, 'Be not afraid; for behold,
I bring you good news of a great joy
which will come to all the people;
for to you is born this day in the city of David a Savior,
who is Christ the Lord.'"
LUKE 2:10,11

It was the worst of all times on a hill outside the Holy City. There the very people Jesus loved and came to rescue and save, held him in derision and nailed him to a cross of agony and torment. It was earth's darkest hour. The sun hid its face for shame. They (and, yes, we sinners were there) tried to get rid of goodness and God. But here we find the best of times!

"But he was wounded for our transgressions,
he was bruised for our iniquities;
upon him was the chastisement that made us whole,
and with his stripes we are healed.
All we like sheep have gone astray;
we have turned every one to his own way;
and the Lord has laid on him the iniquity of us all."
ISAIAH 53:5,6

It was the worst of times for the disciples and followers of Jesus when their Lord was killed. Their hopes died with Him. But it was the best of times on that first Easter morning when the tomb was empty and Jesus came out alive to be with them forever.

"But the angel said to the women, 'Do not be afraid;
for I know that you seek Jesus who was crucified.
He is not here; for he has risen, as he said.
Come, see the place where he lay.'"
MATTHEW 28:5,6

St. Paul writes about the cross in I Corinthians 1:18:

"For the word of the cross is folly to those who are perishing, but to us who are being saved it is the power of God."

St. John the Apostle writes in I John 4:10:

"In this is love, not that we loved God but that he loved us and sent his Son to be the expiation for our sins."

In the book of Revelation we read these words:

"And I heard a loud voice in heaven, saying, 'Now the salvation and the power and the kingdom of our God and the authority of his Christ have come, for the accuser of our brethren has been thrown down, who accuses them day and night before our God. And they have conquered him by the blood of the Lamb and by the word of their testimony, for they loved not their lives even unto death."
REVELATION 12:10,11

Some readers may be asking, "What does this extended message on Jesus and His Calvary love have to do with the title of this book, *Jesus–Final Authority on Marriage and Same-Sex Unions?*" Very much indeed. As we hear about His Calvary love, surely we can accept as Final Authority His Word and Divine Design on the male-female relationship:

"But from the beginning of creation, 'God made them male and female.' 'For this reason a man shall leave his father and mother and be joined to his wife, and the two shall become one flesh.' So they are no longer two but one flesh. What therefore God has joined together, let not man put asunder."
MARK 10:6-9

On that memorable afternoon, Jeff and Moni heard these words, following their vows of love and faithfulness. "For as much as you have been joined in holy wedlock, I as a servant of Jesus Christ, before God and these witnesses, confirm your marriage in the Name of the Father, and of the Son and of the Holy Spirit. Amen."

Marriage in the Divine Design is a miracle. Let me share an example:

Shortly after their engagement, John and Mary were at a pier in New York City. John was ready to board a ship that would take him overseas for a year of military service. Mary was in tears. She clung to John. She said, "I can't let you go. Don't leave me." John tried to comfort Mary, assuring her that they would both make it through the year. Finally, Mary took the ring from her finger and put it on John's finger. She said,, "John, I will let you go on one condition. Promise me that you will never take this ring off until we meet and you put it on my finger. Promise me that as you rub it you will think of me every day." John promised and boarded his ship.

During that year he wrote a daily love letter to Mary. He said, "I bless you for giving me your ring. Because of it, I feel your presence. I am counting the days until I shall take it off, and put it on your finger. I could not have survived without it."

A year later his ship was approaching the New York harbor. John was standing on the top deck. He thought, "In two weeks, after my discharge, I will meet Mary and put this ring back on her finger and we will be together forever." He pictured the scene in his mind. It was so real that he trembled with excitement. Seeking to act out the exciting dream, he removed the ring from his finger. His shaking hand dropped the ring into the ocean. John went into shock. The ring that had sustained him, the ring that he promised never to remove from his finger was gone. And there was nothing he could do about it.

The night before leaving for the west coast reunion, John went into a New York restaurant. He ordered fish for his dinner. In the midst of the meal, he felt a hard object in his mouth. Removing it, he held in his hand–a fish bone! Many years ago when I first heard this story, I was sure that John would be holding the ring in his hand. When I told this story to a group, nearly everyone indicated the same response. I then said, "I am speaking to a wonderful audience. You really believe in miracles!"

For John and Mary, as for Jeff and Moni, the most exciting miracle is the miracle of union by the hand of almighty God. It is called the "one flesh" miracle (Mark 10:6-9). It is the miracle, not of romantic love but of marital love, self-giving love. They love and honor each other so much that they want to share the very best. They share the gift of God's love. The miracle is that they can have His love to share. This says that each one is worthy of the best and highest. The birth of their baby will be more than the fruit of their physical union. It will be a divine miracle.

The wedding ring indeed is a beautiful outward symbol of the lifelong bond and the undying commitment involved in marriage. The cross, however, is **not** a symbol but the reality of the Presence of the Lord. In His Calvary love, He was there to bless Jeff and Moni as husband and wife for His glory and for the welfare of the human family. As they turn to Him, God will continue to bless them with the love of Christ for one another and through the miracle of their marriage remind the world of Christ's self-giving love.

Indeed, this is the Divine Design for marriage.

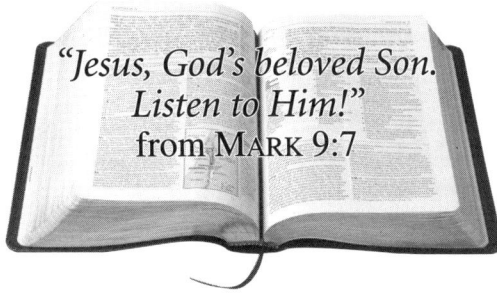

*"Jesus, God's beloved Son.
Listen to Him!"*
from MARK 9:7

Jesus and Our Highest Identity

Because of who He is and who we are in Him, the crisis of identity becomes for us a call to service.

In one of my favorite Bible passages in the Old Testament are the words of King David to his son, Solomon, who was chosen by the God of Israel to build the temple.

> "Be strong and of good courage, and do it.
> Fear not, be not dismayed;
> for the Lord God, even my God, is with you.
> He will not fail you or forsake you until all the work
> for the service of the house of the Lord is finished."
> I CHRONICLES 28:20

Jesus and Our Highest Identity

Arthur Miller, in his famous play entitled, "Death of a Salesman", tells the story of Willie Loman, a salesman, who through many ups and downs, searches in vain to find substantial meaning for his life. These words dramatize the tragedy, " He didn't know who he was."

Our identity, the way in which we view ourselves and the source from which we draw our purpose, is crucial because what we most deeply believe about ourselves directly leads to our behaviors. Indeed, the identity crisis is destroying many persons. A low IQ–Identity Quotient–can lead to destructive behavior. But into this crisis comes Jesus, who not only heals us of our low self-worth malady, but also imparts to all who believe the highest and most hopeful view of who we are and who we are called to be.

You Are More Than You Think

We are more than labels. Labels demean and destroy. We are more than straight or gay persons. We are more than Republicans or Democrats. We are more than liberals or conservatives. Perhaps you have heard someone say, "I like myself just the way I am; just let me be my own person." Is this all that they aspire to be?

In my book, *A Strange Thing Happened to Me on the Way to Retirement–I Never Arrived*, I give other "more than" examples. You are more than your appearance, more than a farmer, more than an athlete, more than a doctor, more than a preacher, more than a homemaker, more than a single person.

And in a fallen world where disease is rampant, we need to remember that we are more than well or sick persons. In St. John's gospel, chapter 11, we find the story of a sick man whose name was Lazarus. Sisters Mary and Martha came to their friend Jesus for help for their brother. They did not say, "Lord, our brother is sick." They said in verse 3, *"Lord, he whom you love is ill."* This is one of the most eloquent and beautiful descriptions of a sick person that one could ever read. It leads from despair to hope. It can help us find meaning in pain and suffering. So let us remember in times of illness that we are more than sick persons. We are sick persons loved by Jesus Christ our Lord and Saviour who can work all things together for good, even illness and pain, for those who put their trust in Him.

Above all, we are more than persons suffering from the world's most deadly disease–sin-sickness. We are sinners loved of God and died for by Jesus, our Saviour. We are redeemed sinners, bought and paid for by the sacrifice of His life for us. Now the question is this: "Will we accept by faith, confession and absolution, who we are and Who He is?"

It's Not Who You Are But <u>Whose</u> You Are, Not What You Do, But What God Has Done

What has God done? Let's take a look at the cross. What are the long rusty spikes piercing the hands and feet of Jesus, the Son of God, saying? "Your sins are nailed to the cross." What is the crown of thorns piercing His holy brow, causing the blood to run like red rubies from a regal crown saying? "I make you worthy to wear the crown of glory forever." What is the robe of ridicule that they put on Jesus saying? "I have a robe of redemption for you which will enable you to stand before the judgment seat, cleansed and righteous." What is the dirty spittle of demonic hatred, running down the holy face of Jesus, saying? "I have for you a radiantly new heart and face in the midst of burdens and sorrow and pain in a fallen world." Jesus' cry of agony from His cross of torture and shame was, *"My God, my God, why hast thou forsaken me?"* What do these words say? "You will never need to walk alone."

It is indeed not who you are but **whose** you are. It is not who you think you are that is important. The crisis question is "Who does Jesus say that you are?" His answer is constant and sure: "You are redeemed! You are a died-for sinner!"

In the Gospel of Luke, chapter 18, we read of a blind man, sitting by the roadside in Jericho. When he heard that Jesus was passing by, he cried out, *"Jesus, Son of David, have mercy on me!"* Many in the crowd rebuked the blind beggar and told him to be silent. He kept on crying and then something happened. Jesus stopped and commanded that the blind man be brought to Him. When the blind man said, *"Lord, let me receive my sight,"* Jesus said to him, *"Receive your sight. Your faith has made you well."* In this man at the side of the road, Jesus saw more than a blind beggar. He saw a man of faith, ready to receive his sight. It is interesting to note that those who were rebuking the blind man for crying out to Jesus were then moved to glorify God because of him. He was no longer a despised blind beggar by the roadside.

Jesus is the great affirmer. Again we refer to the story of Zacchaeus in Luke 19. In verse 9 Jesus says to Zacchaeus, *"Today salvation has come to this house, since he also is a son of Abraham."* Who was He speaking about? Zacchaeus was a despised tax collector and one who cheated people out of their money. But when he met Jesus and heard His affirming words, his life and his deeds were transformed.

In response to Jesus' love of sinners, the Scribes and Pharisees murmured, saying:

> *"This man receives sinners and eats with them."*
> Luke 15:2

We find Jesus' response to them in the parables of The Lost Sheep, The Lost Coin and The Lost Sons. In St. Luke's Gospel, chapter 15, we read the story of "The Two Lost Sons". I think that a more appropriate title for the story would be "The Unconditional Love of the Father".

It is interesting to note in this story that the younger brother, who had spent his inheritance living in debauchery and lust and sins of the flesh came back to his father with a penitent heart, pleading that he might be received as a hired servant. What happened? His overjoyed father arranged for a homecoming celebration. Where was the older brother? He was basking in his spirit of lovelessness and envy and hate for his brother. In the story, the father affirmed his love for the older lost son who stayed home. He said, *"All that is mine is yours."* But that son refused to accept his father's love and affirmation. The younger son who returned chose to accept his identity as a son forgiven and returned to the comfort of his father's home. The older son chose to step away from that identity, choosing an identity of anger and bitterness instead of love.

This brings us to a crisis question.

Who Am I?

Who are you in response to the loving invitation of Jesus? Very often, crises in our lives have a way of stripping us down to these questions. Dietrich Bonhoeffer can help us with the answer. He was a pastor and an instructor in systematic theology at Berlin University during the 1930's. Because of his outspoken opposition to Adolf Hitler, he was arrested, imprisoned and eventually hanged. People who knew him in prison claim that Bonhoeffer was a tower of strength for all of them, a source of inspiration and hope, a dynamic witness for Jesus Christ. Payne Best, an English officer incarcerated with Bonhoeffer said, "Bonhoeffer was one of the very few men that I have ever met to whom his God was real and close."

Yet Dietrich Bonhoeffer saw himself differently. Included in his letters and papers smuggled out of prison is a poem entitled, "Who Am I?" which is found in his book, *Cost of Discipleship*. In that poem he wrote:

"Who am I? They often tell me
I stepped from my cell's confinement
calmly, cheerfully, firmly,
like a squire from his country-house.

Who am I? They often tell me
I used to speak to my warders
freely and friendly and clearly,
as though it were mine to command.

Who am I? They also tell me
I bore the days of misfortune
equably, smilingly, proudly,
like one accustomed to win.

Am I then really all that which other men tell of?
Or am I only what I myself know of myself?
Restless and longing and sick, like a bird in a cage,
struggling for breath, as though hands were compressing my throat,
yearning for colours, for flowers, for the voices of birds,
thirsting for words of kindness, for neighborliness,
tossing in expectation of great events,
powerlessly trembling for friends at infinite distance,
weary and empty at praying, at thinking, at making,
faint, and ready to say farewell to it all?

Who am I? This or the other?
Am I one person to-day and to-morrow another?
Am I both at once? A hypocrite before others,
and before myself a contemptibly woebegone weakling?
Or is something within me still like a beaten army,
fleeing in disorder from victory already achieved?

Who am I? They mock me, these lonely questions of mine.
Whoever I am, Thou knowest, O God, I am thine!"

Dietrich Bonhoeffer asks a question that burns in many hearts today, "Who am I?" In the context of this book, the question for many becomes, "Am I straight or gay?" Another question, "How do I express my human sexuality?" And "Should I reveal my sexual orientation or suffer torment inside?" In these questions, or those of Dietrich Bonhoeffer, or questions of yours and mine, we need to move from "Who am I? to "Whose am I?" Then we can move with hope to our highest identity according to the words of our Creator and Lord:

"But now thus says the Lord, he who created you, O Jacob,
he who formed you, O Israel:

'Fear not, for I have redeemed you;
I have called you by name, you are mine.'"
ISAIAH 43:1

And Jesus has the last word about our highest identity. He said:

"And all of them, since they are mine, belong to you;
and you have given them back to me
with everything else of yours, and so they are my glory!"
JOHN 17:10 (TLB)

Our Highest Identity

Rick Warren, in his book, *The Purpose Driven Life*, reminds us of where the search for our highest identity begins:

"The search for the purpose of life has puzzled people for thousands of years. That's because we typically begin at the wrong starting point–ourselves. We ask self-centered questions like What do *I* want to be? What should *I* do with *my* life? What are *my* goals, *my* ambitions, *my* dreams for *my* future? But focusing on ourselves will never reveal our life's purpose. The Bible says, *'It is God who directs the lives of his creatures; everyone's life is in his power."* (Job 12:10 TEV)

"Contrary to what many popular books, movies, and seminars tell you, you won't discover your life's meaning by looking within yourself. You've probably tried that already. You didn't create yourself, so there is no way you can tell yourself what you were created for! If I handed you an invention you had never seen before, you wouldn't know its purpose, and the invention itself wouldn't be able to tell you either. Only the creator or the owner's manual could reveal its purpose."

So we continue the search for our highest identity. We will find it in our Highest Authority:

"But to all who received him, who believed in his name,
he gave power to become children of God;

*who were born, not of blood nor of the will of the flesh
nor of the will of man, but of God.*
JOHN 1:12,13

*"In him, according to the purpose of him
who accomplishes all things according to the counsel of his will,
we who first hoped in Christ have been destined and appointed
to live for the praise of his glory "*
EPHESIANS 1:11,12

*"For we are his workmanship,
created in Christ Jesus for good works,
which God prepared beforehand,
that we should walk in them."*
EPHESIANS 2:10

We can also learn something about our highest identity from the story of a young boat builder. Johnny spent many months of his spare time building a toy boat. He followed the manual carefully. It was larger than most toy boats, over six feet long. Meticulously, he glued the tiny pieces and the large pieces together. One day Johnny and his father went to the shore of the river flowing near their home. Johnny tied a cord to his boat and ran along the shore pulling his boat in the water. The boat sailed upright, perfectly balanced, a great sight to behold. Johnny tripped as he was running, and as his father was attending to him, the boat was carried to the center of the river and disappeared around the bend. The next day after Johnny had recovered from his fall, he and his father searched up and down the river in a motor boat, but they found no trace of his boat. Johnny was heartbroken.

Several weeks later, Johnny and his father were walking in the downtown area of their town. Suddenly, Johnny shouted, "Look, Daddy!" And he pointed to the display window of a store. There on a stand was his boat. There was a sign in the window that read, "For sale, $200." Johnny and his father rushed in and explained to the store keeper about Johnny's boat, and how glad they were to find it again. Johnny said, "Can I please have my boat?" The salesman said, "We bought this boat from a stranger recently and paid him for it. You can have this boat for $200."

As Johnny cried, his father, a very wise man, said, "Johnny, I will loan you the $200 you need. You will have plenty of time to pay me back doing odd jobs."

As Johnny's father held the boat, Johnny wrote on its side, "This boat belongs to Johnny." As they left the store, Johnny held the boat high and said, "Now you really belong to me. You belong to me for three reasons. First, I made you with my own hands. Then when you got lost I bought you back. And now my name is written on you."

Here we have three reasons that reveal why every reader of this book and every person in the world is of infinite and priceless worth. First, God created us in His image and likeness. Indeed He created everything that exists, but we are His highest creation.

Second, when we became lost in sin, separated from our Creator-God, destined to live meaningless and futile lives, our Lord would not let His people stay lost. He redeemed us, bought us back, paying the price of our redemption with His own life, even as His body was nailed to a cross of torture and shame.

Oswald Chambers, in his book *My Utmost for His Highest*, comments on Redemption:

> "All through the Bible it is revealed that Our Lord bore the sin of the world by *identification*, not by *sympathy*. He deliberately took upon His own shoulders, and bore in His own Person, the whole massed sin of the human race–'He hath *made Him to be sin for us*, who knew no sin,' and by so doing He put the whole human race on the basis of Redemption. Jesus Christ rehabilitated the human race; He put it back to where God designed it to be, and anyone can enter into union with God on the ground of what Our Lord has done on the Cross."

"For our sake he made him to be sin who knew no sin,
so that in him we might become the righteousness of God."
II CORINTHIANS 5:21

Some persons harbor the strange belief that if you call yourself a sinner you are putting yourself down. In reality, we are being lifted up into the highest designation and honor that any person could receive. It is that of "redeemed sinner", "sinner-saint", "died-for and bought-back sinner", "forgiven sinner", "a new person in Christ, destined to be like Him".

Third, just as Johnny wrote on his boat, "This boat belongs to Johnny," so we belong to Him. As a divine sign and guarantee of this belonging, He has chosen us to be indwelt by the Holy Spirit. This means that the presence of Jesus Himself is with us and within us:

> *"Do you not know that your body is the temple*
> *of the Holy Spirit within you, which you have from God?*
> *You are not your own; you were bought with a price.*
> *So glorify God in your body."*
> I CORINTHIANS 6:19,20

> *"By this we know that we abide in him and he in us,*
> *because he has given us of his own Spirit."*
> I JOHN 4:13

How can persons who know that they are sinners possibly accept themselves as children of the King of Kings with all the rights and privileges of living in His kingdom?

Max Lucado, in his book *Grace for the Moment*, will help answer this question. He begins with a scripture passage:

> *"We Christians actually do have within us*
> *a portion of the very thoughts and mind of Christ."*
> I CORINTHIANS 2:16 (TLB)

"The distance between our hearts and (Jesus' heart) seems so immense. How could we ever hope to have the heart of Jesus?

"Ready for a surprise? You already do. . . . If you are in Christ, you already have the heart of Christ. One of the supreme yet unrealized promises of God is simply this: if you have given your life to Jesus, Jesus has given himself to you.

He has made your heart his home. It would be hard to say it more succinctly than Paul does: 'Christ lives in me' (Gal. 2:20 MSG). . . .

"He has moved in and unpacked his bags and is ready to change you 'into his likeness from one degree of glory to another' (2 Cor. 3:18 RSV)."

How can heterosexuals, struggling with lust and infidelity, and homosexuals, aching for guidance for their sexual behavior, accept themselves as redeemed and beloved children of God? A reassuring answer is given in Galatians 2:20:

> *"I have been crucified with Christ;*
> *it is no longer I who live, but Christ who lives in me;*
> *and the life I now live in the flesh I live by faith*
> *in the Son of God, who loved me and gave himself for me."*

In Jesus, then, we find our highest Identity.

Living In Our Highest Identity

Having been affirmed by our Lord as forgiven sinners, cleansed and made righteous in the blood of Jesus, do we live in and then act upon that identity? Do we affirm others in Christ? Are we Ministers of Affirmation?

It is possible, of course, to engage in "affirmation with an angle". This means giving shallow compliments that can reflect an ego trip, "Look how friendly I am." It is possible also to affirm persons in their destructive life styles. Though this seems easier for the moment, our words do not bear the love that only truth can bring.

Recognizing our high and holy calling as Ministers of Affirmation can be a safeguard against chronic complaining, a devastating practice indeed. It seems especially easy to complain and to criticize those whom we say we love. It is often tragically true that we wait until the Memorial Service to magnify a loved one's life and works. It is always possible to affirm someone in Christ, or in what we know they can become in Christ and will become as they are prayed for.

My life partner, Marta, was a beautiful Minister of Affirmation. I recall holding our six-month-old son Billy in my arms. A lady came up to me and said, "Is that your grandson?" This gave me dark and negative thoughts. How could she think I am the grandfather? I said to Marta, "Do you think I look a lot older?" She replied, "No, sweetheart, you just look more mature!"

Marta was very patient with me when my sermons were too long. Following a message at a youth gathering on a college campus, I recall Marta saying, "You preached two good sermons today!" Can we find something positive about any person, even with the knowledge that there are many things radically wrong in that person's life? It can be a challenge, but one we must enter if we are to carry the grace-giving Spirit of Christ.

You surely will not find many "Ministers of Defamation" among those whom Jesus has affirmed with His unconditional and forgiving love. Jesus specializes in changing failures like us into new persons leading fruitful and abundant lives. In many church bodies today, there is debate and controversy over the ordination of men and women living in same-sex unions. Someone will probably say, "Well, is not this an example of Christian affirmation of persons expressing their human sexuality according to their needs and orientation?" But such human affirmation is revealed to be false in the light of the clear teachings of Jesus regarding the man-woman relationship in marriage. Again, we hear the words of truth spoken by Jesus:

> *"But from the beginning of creation, 'God made them male and female.' 'For this reason, a man shall leave his father and mother and be joined to his wife, and the two shall become one flesh.' So they are no longer two but one. What therefore God has joined together, let not man put asunder."*
>
> MARK 10:6-9

Fully accepted in the love of God and fully grounded in His truth, our identity stops being a cause for crisis but instead becomes a cause for celebration.

In one of my favorite Bible passages in the Old Testament are the words of King David to his son, Solomon, who was chosen by the God of Israel to build the temple:

"Be strong and of good courage, and do it.
Fear not, be not dismayed;
for the Lord God, even my God, is with you.
He will not fail you or forsake you until all the work
for the service of the house of the Lord is finished."
I CHRONICLES 28:20

This is high affirmation of us sinners. The task He assigns may sound impossible, but He has created us, redeemed us and sealed us with His own Spirit to equip us for His work. And he has promised to be with us to fulfill the service He has chosen for us.

We find an eloquent word of affirmation for all who receive their identity in Christ in John 15:16 (NKJV):

"You did not choose me, but I chose you
and appointed you that you should go and bear fruit
and that your fruit should abide;
that whatever you ask of the father in my name,
he may give it to you."

Thanks be to God for His gifts of life-giving, life-sharing identity and divine affirmation!

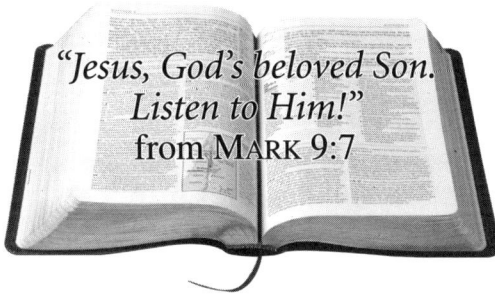

*"Jesus, God's beloved Son.
Listen to Him!"*
from MARK 9:7

Jesus is Lord
of the Church

I am an incurable optimist about the Church. Yes, the Church, with its apostasy, betrayals, confusion, compromises and sins, a Church filled with sinners like me in it! How can I help but be optimistic about the Church when I remember that I belong to an Unshakable Kingdom and to Jesus, Lord of the Church!

"Therefore let us be grateful for receiving a kingdom that cannot be shaken, and thus let us offer to God acceptable worship, with reverence and awe; for our God is a consuming fire."
HEBREWS 12:28-29

Jesus is Lord of the Church

In writing on a controversial issue in the Church and society, I have tried to display a positive, hopeful and non-judgmental spirit and perspective. In fact, in this final chapter, I hope to be pictured as an incurable optimist.How can I be optimistic about the Church, filled as it is with its apostasy, betrayals, confusion, compromises–a Church filled with sinners like me? My answer is, "How can I help but be optimistic about the Church when I remember the words of Jesus in Matthew 16?" Here we find the answer to His question to His disciples, "Who do men say that the Son of Man is?" Their answers included John the Baptist, Elijah, Jeremiah or one of the prophets. Then Jesus said to them, "But who do you say that I am?" Simon Peter answered, "You are the Christ, the Son of the living God." Then Jesus answered him in Matthew 16:17,18:

> *"Blessed are you, Simon Bar-Jona!*
> *For flesh and blood has not revealed this to you,*
> *but my Father who is in heaven.*
> *And I tell you, you are Peter,*
> *and on this rock I will build my church,*
> *and the powers of death shall not prevail against it.'"*

Indeed, I can be optimistic about the Church when I remember that He is the foundation:

> *For no other foundation can any one lay than that which is laid,*
> *which is Jesus Christ."*
> I CORINTHIANS 3:11

In the Church of Jesus Christ, I belong to an Unshakable Kingdom and to an Unchanging Person who calls me to worship with reverence and awe:

"Therefore let us be grateful for receiving a kingdom
that cannot be shaken, and thus let us offer
to God acceptable worship, with reverence and awe;
for our God is a consuming fire.
HEBREWS 12:28-29

Here is another question. How can I be optimistic about the Church in our fallen world which is enemy-occupied territory? Here, the Church is under siege by the enemies of the Cross of Christ. Here we face crime, violence, wars, revolutions, terrorism, paganism, and not least, a sexual revolution that threatens to destroy our nation. I should add that at the time this is written, my country is engaged in military, political and spiritual warfare. Indeed, it is "tough going" for the Church in this world.

But I am optimistic about the Church because I am also optimistic about our world as I recall the words of Jesus:

"For God so loved the world that he gave his only Son,
that whoever believes in him should not perish but have eternal life."
JOHN 3:16

I take courage when I remember that this is the world God loves. He came to this fallen world in the person of His Son. Jesus was nailed to a cruel cross that we might become the righteousness of God in Him. Indeed we are under Divine judgment in this world but also under Divine love, greater than our sins.

God loved the world so much! He is at work in His world, redeeming, healing, sustaining, renewing and upholding His children until He brings all things into subjection to Himself. Because of God's love in Jesus, we can live in this world with an unshakable optimism. Then we will praise Him for all the great things He is doing in His Church and in His world.

"O sing to the Lord a new song, for he has done marvelous things!
His right hand and his holy arm have gotten him victory."
PSALM 98:1

We are also optimistic about the future. For in Jesus we have hope for life and for Eternal Life. Marta Berg, a radiant optimist, writes about this hope in a poem entitled "Home" from her book, *From Grey to Gold*:

"High above Denmark's great harbor,
I learned a new truth.

Always I had thought that birds
belong to the realm of sky,
for we look up to see them.

But, no,
as the great plane thundered its way upward and onward,
I saw that birds belong to the kingdom of Earth, not sky.
Earth is where their homing instinct
takes them.

At day's end,
unerringly,
they go for home, the Earth.
Why is it that man oftentimes
feels out of place, and flounders about,
alienated,
in this, his Father's world?

Perhaps it is that
he doesn't know
the Father.

He doesn't know that he is a child of the universe,
and that in the Father-Creator,
all things are interrelated.

No one is ever alone."

Never alone! We remember His promise:

". . .I will never leave you or forsake you."
HEBREWS 13:5 (NKJV)

A Reality Check for the Church

Many years ago I attended a meeting of national Directors of Evangelism of nine Lutheran Church bodies. Dr. Oswald Waech, Director of Evangelism of the Lutheran Church, Missouri Synod, told us of his fourth-grade daughter coming to school one morning and finding the teacher distraught and upset. She said, "Children, some very wicked people have done all this awful damage that you see–broken windows, garbage on our lawn, our beautiful flowers destroyed. We call these bad people vandals, and the evil things they do, we call vandalism." She went on and on about this evil. Dr. Waech's little daughter raised her hand and said loudly and proudly, "Teacher, my Daddy's director of vandalism!"

Serving as Director of Evangelism for my national Church for eleven years, I am reminded that there is a fine line, easy to step over, between vandalism and evangelism. Confession of the Christian faith without commitment to Christ and His work of redemption is a form of vandalism. It is vandalism when we seek members for what they can put into the church in terms of institutional support instead of what God can put into them in terms of new life and hope. It is vandalism when the Christian gospel is exchanged for the doctrine of cheap grace and universalism. It is vandalism to exchange the truth of God for a lie (Romans 1:25). It is vandalism when we steal joy and the sense of dignity and worth from anyone, not least from those struggling with their human sexuality. It is vandalism to reduce the teaching of scripture to accommodate a political, personal or social agenda.

The reality of spiritual vandalism in our world today is prevalent and deepens our need in the Church for highlighting true evangelism and missions as never before. We are called to be the presence of Christ in the world, the peace of Christ where there is no peace. This we can accomplish only as Christ lives in us.

Submission to the Lord of the Church means that we are willing to pay the price of membership in His Church. Our Lord paid the price by suffering agony on His cross of torture and shame to become the rock and foundation of our salvation. Likewise, it is costly for us to become members of His Church. In the light of the "divine cost", the casual commitment and nominalism of many in the Church appear as "cheap grace" and as completely unworthy of the name, "Christian".

Dietrich Bonhoeffer in his book, *The Cost of Discipleship*, gives a much needed reminder:

> "Cheap grace is the preaching of forgiveness without requiring repentance, baptism without Church discipline, Communion without confession, absolution without contrition. Cheap grace is grace without discipleship, grace without the Cross, grace without Jesus Christ, living and incarnate."

Bonhoeffer also writes about "costly grace":

> "Such grace is *costly* because it calls us to follow, and it is grace because it calls us to follow *Jesus Christ*. It is costly because it costs a man his life, and it is grace because it gives a man the only true life. It is costly because it condemns sin, and grace because it justifies the sinner. Above all, it is costly because it cost God the life of His Son: 'ye were bought at a price,' and 'what has cost God much cannot be cheap for us.'"

We are living stones built into a spiritual house, but it is costly. It is costly in terms of surrender to the builder and His plans:

> *"Come to him, to that living stone,*
> *rejected by men but in God's sight chosen and precious;*
> *and like living stones be yourselves built into a spiritual house,*
> *to be a holy priesthood, to offer spiritual sacrifices*
> *acceptable to God through Jesus Christ."*
> I Peter 2:4-6

Whose house is it? Whose Church is it? In Matthew 16:18, Jesus says, "Upon this rock, I will build **my** church." I recall the story of a traveling salesman who came to a small town on a Sunday morning.

He asked a man sitting on a porch swing, "Can you tell me where Christ Church is?" The man scratched his head and said, "Well, I know there's John Courtney's church downtown; there's Father John's Catholic Church on the edge of town; there's Sister Fern's Tabernacle on Fifth Street–come to think of it, stranger, I don't think Christ has a church in this town!"

I am sure that we intend no theological aberrations when we speak of "my church" or ask, "which is your church". However, there are ominous indications that many in the church are acting as if it was their church. They decide what is right and wrong as they make decisions about church membership. This brings us back to the title of this book, *Jesus–Final Authority on Marriage and Same-Sex Unions.* I believe we are asking an incongruous question when we say, "Shall we bless same-sex unions?" It would seem that this is an effort to make the Church over into our own human image and likeness. Jesus is the Head of the Church, the Founder of the Church, the Sustainer of the Church and its Foundation. He is the one who decides whom to bless and who does the blessing.

The Church and Its Word and Sacrament Ministry

I am optimistic about the Church when I think of its Word and Sacrament ministry. The Church is the place where Jesus first met me, cleansed me and claimed me for His own Family. Because of Jesus, I am able to be optimistic about myself even though I am, according to Martin Luther's explanation in the second article of our faith, "a lost and condemned creature". I believe that Jesus Christ has "redeemed me, secured and delivered me from all sins, from death and from the power of the devil." As I continue to experience the reality of God's redeeming work in me each day, I also know that the Church will continue to be redeemed and renewed and remain a place where others can begin their life in Christ, just as I did. Indeed, the Church is a place of beginnings.

God begins His holy pursuit of us as soon as we are born. In the Lutheran Church, we practice infant baptism. I have often thought that Baptism is the Gospel of Grace in its purest form. A baby is not guilty of sinful acts but has inherited a sinful nature. Before the child has the capacity to ask for divine help, the Lord comes to cleanse the child from all sin by His indwelling presence.

Infant baptism and adult conversion belong together. An inner change does take place in baptism. This comes by the regenerating power of the Holy Spirit through God's Word. God's love is poured into a helpless sinner who cannot lift a finger toward his or her salvation. But infant baptism must emerge into a conscious acknowledgment of Jesus Christ as Saviour and Lord–into a willingness to be changed by the transforming power of the indwelling Holy Spirit. Somewhere along the line after my baptism as an infant, I must come to the place of accepting God's acceptance of me. We read in Matthew 28:19,20:

> *"Go therefore and make disciples of all nations, baptizing them*
> *in the name of the Father and of the Son and of the Holy Spirit,*
> *teaching them to observe all that I have commanded you;*
> *and lo, I am with you always, to the close of the age."*

In this passage we have a safeguard against "automatic salvation". Parents, sponsors and the fellowship of believers in the Church are called to bring up the child in the nurture and admonition of the Lord. This means instruction in the Christian faith and training in obedience to God's commandments. Thus they are enabled to keep what they have received from their Lord in Holy Baptism. In the Baptismal Service in the Evangelical Lutheran Church in America, we find these words: "Child of God, you have been sealed by the Holy Spirit and marked with the Cross of Christ forever." What a high and memorable moment in a child's life! And for parents and family, that precious mark, standing for the unconditional love of our Lord and Saviour, also calls for responsibility and accountability.

When our son Bill was baptized, I shall never forget a vision that came to me, and stays with me now over fifty years later. I saw the angels of God in a celebration of praise, about to welcome Bill into the Kingdom of God.

I also saw another angel writing the words, William John Berg, in the Book of Life. Holy Baptism! It's something to celebrate!

There is another experience that happens in the Church that gives me hope and optimism. We call it the Sacrament of the Altar, Holy Communion, the Eucharist. Here I can kneel at the Holy Altar in the Lord's Sanctuary or among believers and saints in other places. I can hear the story from Matthew 26:26-28:

> *"Now as they were eating, Jesus took bread,*
> *and blessed, and broke it, and gave it to the disciples*
> *and said, 'Take, eat; this is my body.'*
> *And he took a cup, and when he had given thanks*
> *he gave it to them, saying, 'Drink of it, all of you;*
> *for this is my blood of the covenant,*
> *which is poured out for many for the forgiveness of sins.'"*

This is a very personal experience. Jesus says, "For you" as we receive his sacrifice. Yet, I do not kneel at the altar alone. I am strengthened by the presence of brothers and sisters who kneel beside me. I cannot make it to the Promised Land alone. I am part of a great company of travelers. We share struggles, suffering and burdens as well as joys and victories, inspiring one another to go on.

Each time that I am on my way to the altar for Holy Communion, I am singing in my spirit the song:

"Just as I am, without one plea,
But that thy blood was shed for me,
And that thou bidd'st me come to thee,
O Lamb of God, I come, I come.

"Just as I am, thou wilt receive,
Wilt welcome, pardon, cleanse, relieve;
Because thy promise I believe,
O Lamb of God, I come, I come."

Indeed, the Lutheran Church has an Altar Call for penitent sinners!

In Holy Communion, we gather at the Altar of God to be transformed. God speaks of this change when he says:

"I beseech you therefore, brethren, by the mercies of God,
that you present your bodies a living sacrifice,
holy, acceptable unto God, which is your reasonable service.
And be not conformed to this world,
but be transformed by the renewing of your mind,
that you may prove what is that good and acceptable
and perfect will of God."
ROMANS 12:1,2

On His final night on earth with those He loved, Christ instituted Holy Communion as an experience of remembrance to which we should continuously return. We remember that we have received mercy. We remember that we have been called together as the people of God and that He is our common bond, not we ourselves. The Church is a place of divine togetherness.

In 1936 I was serving as a student intern in a large congregation in Chicago, Illinois. A member of the congregation was wheeled into the operating room of the hospital for critical surgery. These were the days before blood banks were available. I was wheeled on a cot into the operating room. My cot was placed alongside my friend on the operating table. Blood flowed directly from my body into her body. Her health was restored following successful surgery. It was indeed an impressive moment for me as I was assisting at the altar of her Church at a Communion Service. As she knelt there, how true it was that my blood was life for her physically. And blood, the shed blood of Jesus from a cross, was new life for her spiritually! Indeed, we might say that Holy Communion brings to us the Divine Blood Transfusion.

My optimism for the Church increases when I remember that I am baptized, sealed by the Holy Spirit and marked by the sign of the Cross. I am called with others to be a guest at the Banquet Table of the King. No wonder that I am grateful for the Church and optimistic about her future under the divine blessing and guidance of Jesus, Lord of the Church.

The Church Is Without Walls

When I think of the Church in the world, the Church without

walls, I can get truly excited about the Church and its ministries. In the two inner-city churches that it was my privilege to serve, our understanding of the Church as existing primarily for those outside the fellowship helped to guide us in our ministries. This statement no doubt startles many church members. But it has always been clear to me that the Lord gathers us together in the place of worship. There, by the power of the Holy Spirit, we are prepared to be soldiers of the cross in the world.

In the vestibule of the Augustana Lutheran Church in Minneapolis, Minnesota, it is difficult for exiting worshippers to miss the sign, "The Worship is Over, the Service Begins". The Holy Spirit is power for the accomplishment of this service .

A request for the gift and power of the Holy Spirit is a way of saying that we are willing to get involved in what He is doing in the world. It is a commitment to action in the ministry of healing and reconciliation for all persons. Indeed, there is no point in praying for the Holy Spirit unless we are willing to assume responsibility in meeting human need in the world. I John 3:18 says to us:

> *"Little children, let us not love in word or speech*
> *but in deed and in truth."*

It is important to note that love heads the list of the fruit of the Spirit (Galations 5:22). In his book, *Growing Spiritually*, E. Stanley Jones writes:

> "If we grow in love, then we grow. If we don't grow, then we simply go, not grow. And it is a very barren going. . .
>
> "We remain immature if we are immature in our love. If the love is ingrown, centering on itself as the focus of its love, then the result is an immature personality. If the love is selectedly applied to certain groups and classes and races, again the result is an immature personality. . .
>
> "And modern discoveries in psychology would agree with this conclusion. Dr. Karl Menninger, the famous psychiatrist, was asked at a forum what one was to do if he felt a nervous

breakdown coming on. You would have thought that he would have replied, 'Go to a psychiatrist, but instead he replied: 'Lock up your house, go across the railway tracks and find someone in need, and do something for him.'"

Indeed, the Church is without walls!

Where Is The Church

A classic definition of the Church is found in Luther's catechism: "Wherever the Word is preached in its truth and purity, and the sacraments are administered according to the Word and institution of Christ." We learn more specifically from the Word of God where the Church is. The Church is:

Where we worship in spirit and in truth:

"O come, let us worship and bow down,
let us kneel before the Lord, our maker."
PSALM 95:6

Where we preach the Gospel of Jesus Christ for salvation and service:

"For what we preach is not ourselves, but Jesus Christ as Lord,
with ourselves as your servants for Jesus' sake."
II CORINTHIANS 4:5

Where we teach the Word of God for spiritual growth:

". . .teaching them to observe all that I have commanded you;
and lo, I am with you always, to the close of the age."
MATTHEW 28:20

Where we reach people everywhere with healing love for body and spirit:

"Jesus said, 'They need not go away;
you give them something to eat.'"
MATTHEW 14:16

What Is The Church

We need to review and re-study the nature and mission of the Church.

It is created by the Holy Spirit for holy purposes.

It exists by divine power through the means of grace.

It is God's reconciling and redemptive mission in every community.

It is the people of God, gathered at the Cross, equipped by the Spirit and scattered in the world as His servants and witnesses.

"But you shall receive power
when the Holy Spirit has come upon you;
and you shall be my witnesses in Jerusalem
and in all Judea and Samaria and to the end of the earth."
ACTS 1:8

What is the Work of the Church?

As we review the nature and mission of the Church, let us consider some thought-starters as we seek to fulfill the work of evangelism.

Evangelism without fanaticism.
Urgency without frenzy.
Proclamation without manipulation.
Promotion without pressure.
Enthusiasm without theological naivete.
Personal regeneration with social concern.
    John 3:16 with I John 3:16.

It is not an occupation–rather, an outcome.
It is not a profession–rather, an obsession.
It is not by method–rather, by contagion.
It is not by human power–rather, "by my Spirit".

Is it something you do?–Or something He has done.
Are they our plans?–Or His passion.

105

Is it human aspiration?–Or Divine revelation.
Are they blueprints of a plan?–Or Footprints of a Person.
Is it regimentation?–Or regeneration.
Is it a system of thought?–Or a Saviour of persons.

The Church–a Place for the Great Exchange

Your Emptiness for His Fullness–John 1:16
Your Reluctance for His Willingness–Psalm 91:15,16
Your Sin for His Grace–Romans 5:20
Your Bondage for His Freedom–John 8:31,32
Your Loneliness for His Presence–John 14:18
Your "Why?" for His "Why?"–Psalm 42:9,11
Your Wounded Heart for His Wounds–Isaiah 53:4,5
Your Burdens for His Blessings–Matthew 11:28
Your Aches for His Word of Assurance–Romans 8:28,32
Your Call for Help for His Deliverance–Psalm 50:15
Your Lamentation for His Praise–Lamentations 3:20-23

This is indeed the world's greatest Exchange Counter:

> *"Therefore, since we are surrounded by so great a cloud of witnesses, let us also lay aside every weight, and sin which clings so closely, and let us run with perseverance the race that is set before us, looking to Jesus the pioneer and perfecter of our faith, who for the joy that was set before him endured the cross, despising the shame, and is seated at the right hand of the throne of God."*
> HEBREWS 12:1,2

Now we face a recurring question, "What does this review of the mission of the Church have to do with the title of this book, *Jesus– Final Authority on Marriage and Same-Sex Unions?*" No doubt many who are living in same-sex unions, longing for the blessing of the Church on them, will agree in general with my picture of the Church. So what is the problem? The problem is a confusion of voices expressing varying interpretations of Scripture. We need to listen to the voice of the Lord of the Church. On every chapter title page of this book we read the words, "Listen to Him". Here again are His words on the man and woman relationship in marriage:

> *"But from the beginning of creation, 'God made them male and female.' 'For this reason a man shall leave his father and mother and be joined to his wife, and the two shall become one flesh.' So they are no longer two but one flesh. What therefore God has joined together, let not man put asunder."*
>
> MARK 10:6-9

The Church and Its Call to Evangelism

During the decade of 1950-60, some 15,000 congregations in nine Lutheran Church bodies participated in Evangelism Missions, also known as Preaching-Teaching-Reaching Missions. One of the most significant features of this program was preparing lay visitors to call on church members and the unchurched on the congregation's "responsibility list", to befriend, invite and to share their faith. Participation at these missions throughout the church ranged from areas of eight congregations in small towns to three hundred congregations in the Chicago-land Mission. Thousands of parish pastors served as "guest missioners".

It is true that statistics cannot accurately measure spiritual progress. However, the following statistics from this mission can be a challenge for us: 20,800 lay visitors were commissioned, 96,700 church members and 45,000 unchurched persons were visited. Of these, 10,000 made commitments for baptism and membership.

During this decade, the participating church bodies reported increases in church membership from two to five per cent.

A major concern should be the "danger of distraction". Will the Church-wide controversy on the blessing of same-sex unions make the focus on the central mission of the Church unclear? Will human prejudices and passions distract us from the passion of Jesus? Will the call for change be heard above the call to the great commission of our Lord to *"Go and make disciples, baptizing and teaching them?"* Teaching them what? *"To observe all that he has commanded."* (Matthew 28:19,20).

It is time to ask, "Who is eligible for the blessing of the Lord?" One answer is given in Psalm 67:1,2:

> *"May God be gracious to us and bless us*
> *and make his face to shine upon us,*
> *that thy way may be known on earth,*
> *thy saving power among all nations."*

His blessing and His call to make known His way are inseparable. Is there any more urgent time than now, in our day of grace, for all of us blessed ones to rise up and heed the call of the Lord of the Church to His mission in the world?

Today, something is happening in the Evangelical Lutheran Church in America that increases my OQ, Optimism Quotient. In the National Assembly of the Church held in the summer of 2003, voting members adopted a comprehensive evangelism strategy for the Church. The title for this ministry is, "Sharing Faith in a New Century: A Vision for Evangelism in the ELCA." The assembly commended the plan for "study and implementation" throughout this Church and affirmed its four significant objectives: calling the Church to prayer, preparing and renewing evangelical leaders, teaching discipleship and renewing congregations.

In a recent issue of the ELCA publication, *The Lutheran,* our Presiding Bishop, Mark S. Hanson, wrote a powerful and challenging message that gave me a new surge of hope for my Church:

> "What images come to mind when you hear the word *fire?* A gentle campfire offering warmth and conversation with friends? A raging fire devouring forests and homes? Flickering candles on a cake, marking the passing of years? Acolytes processing with torches, calling our hearts to the One who is the center of worship, Christ, the light of the world? Tongues of fires descending upon that diverse assembly gathered in Jerusalem on Pentecost?

"Images of fire permeate our language, stirring fear and fascination. For those who have experienced fire's destructive power, the memories never go away. For those who have seen new growth in a charred forest, fire has provided occasion for hope. And who has not been drawn into contemplation or rest sitting before a fire?

"What stirs the flames in us? What images of fire would you use to describe the life and ministry of your congregation, your synod, the ELCA?

"In an increasingly diverse world, are we a Pentecost church in which people hear and understand one another telling of God's mighty deeds, each in their own language? Are we on fire, eager to share the good news of Jesus the Christ and to work for justice and peace? Or do we prefer congregations where we can gather around the hearth to experience the warmth of belonging?

"Is it the light of the crucified and risen Christ that illumines the darkness of our lives, or are we drawn to the glitzy lights of our consumer culture to drive despair and sin away? Or are we a church being consumed by smoldering fires of resentment, distrust and alienation?

"John the Baptist speaks of fire as the life-giving power of God that comes through Christ: 'I baptize you with water; but the one who is more powerful than I is coming. . . . he will baptize you with the Holy Spirit and fire' (Luke 3:16). Jesus claimed that power, announcing, 'I come to bring fire to the earth, and how I wish it were already kindled' (Luke 12:49)."

In anticipation of the ELCA Assembly in 2005, **I hope and pray for an overwhelming vote that affirms marriage according to scripture and according to Jesus and His Divine Design.** If this happens, we will be free to focus on the church-wide evangelism emphasis under the theme, "Sharing Faith in a New Century–A Vision for Evangelism in the ELCA". This could lead us into one of the finest and most fruitful eras in the history of our Church.

I also hope and pray that the decision of the Assembly will not make provision for some congregations to affirm and bless same-sex unions which are the "equivalent of marriage". Such compromise and confusion would make the ELCA worthy of censure.

And how do we close this time of reflection on the Divine Design? With a prayer to God to enable His Church to receive by faith His design and His love that it embodies:

> *"I do not cease to give thanks for you, remembering you in my prayers, that the God of our Lord Jesus Christ, the Father of glory, may give you a spirit of wisdom and of revelation in the knowledge of him, having the eyes of your hearts enlightened, that you may know what is the hope to which he has called you, what are the riches of his glorious inheritance in the saints, and what is the immeasurable greatness of his power in us who believe, according to the working of his great might which he accomplished in Christ when he raised him from the dead and made him sit at his right hand in the heavenly places, far above all rule and authority and power and dominion, and above every name that is named, not only in this age but also in that which is to come; and he has put all things under his feet and has made him the head over all things for the church, which is his body, the fullness of him who fills all in all."*
>
> EPHESIANS 1:16-23

How do we thank our Lord for His Church? Surely, by our lips speaking His Word of truth, by our lives lived according to His Divine Plan for us:

> *"Now to him who by the power at work within us*
> *is able to do far more abundantly than all that we ask or think,*
> *to him be glory in the church and in Christ Jesus*
> *to all generations, for ever and ever. Amen."*
>
> EPHESIANS 3:20,21

"And my God will supply every need of yours
according to his riches in glory in Christ Jesus."
<small>PHILIPPIANS</small> 4:19

All glory to Him who will supply every need of ours in Christ Jesus!

Thank You

To the publisher of this book, Lutheran Colportage Service of Minneapolis, Minnesota. For 70 years, this center has been publishing the good news of divine love across the city, nation and world. And more–across inner-city streets in personal evangelism and social ministries. I am happy to have the Lutheran Colportage Service symbol of the flame and cross on this book.

To my family whose love, support and prayers have been an indispensable part of this writing ministry. Their moral support, together with their generous investment of time in the editing process, have given me a big lift along the way.

To countless friends who have been praying for me, and who have affirmed me in this ministry by their oft-repeated words, "We are looking forward to reading your book."

To Marta Berg, my life partner for 55 years. Her poems, her brilliant mind and beautiful spirit are indeed reflected brightly in this book. In 1996, she became one of the Saints in Glory.

To Dr. Theodore E. Conrad, college and seminary professor, scholar and theologian and friend, who at age 99 carries on fruitful ministries from his wheelchair, blessing me in our many visits. He is quoted in this book.

To Perry Duff Smith, Jr., a specialist in the field of graphic design who captures the message of the book in his special art cover. He is also the layout artist. His professional guidance in the long journey toward publication has given me confidence and assurance.

To Carol Smith for her typing of the manuscript and her editing skills. She has shown patience and poise under the pressure of deadlines and has spent hours as a research specialist in securing copyright privileges.

Acknowledgments

Taken from "A Tale of Two Trains", a sermon delivered August 17, 2003 by Coleman Tyler at Galilee Episcopal Church, Virginia Beach, Virginia. Used by permission (pages xii, 24).

Taken from *Mahatma Gandhi* by E. Stanley Jones. Copyright © MCMXLVIII by Stone & Pierce. Used by permission of Abingdon Press (page 4).

Taken from *Jesus Stands Alone!* by Dr. Gordon C. Hunter. Copyright © by Gordon C. Hunter. Used by permission of Anna Hunter on behalf of the original publisher, Christian Discovery, Inc. (pages 6-8).

Taken from *In Christ* by E. Stanley Jones. Copyright © 1961 by Abingdon Press. Used by permission of Abingdon Press (page 8).

Taken from *I Believe in the Church* by Dr. Conrad Bergendoff. Copyright © 1937 by Augustana Book Concern. Used by permission of Augsburg Fortress (pages 8-10).

Taken from *Seen and Unseen* by Marta Berg. Copyright © 1991 by Marta Berg. Winston-Derek Publishers, Inc. (pages 14-15, 34-35, 59-60).

Taken from *The Way* by E. Stanley Jones. Copyright © 1946 by Stone & Pierce. Copyright renewal 1974 by Mable Lossing Jones. Published by Abingdon Press in 1991 as an Abingdon Classic. Used by permission of Abingdon Press (pages 18-20).

Taken from "The Church and Human Sexuality, a Lutheran Perspective", written by Members of the Luther Seminary Faculty, October, 1993. Used by permission (pages 22-23).

Taken from *My Utmost for His Highest* by Oswald Chambers. Copyright © 1935 by Dodd Mead & Co., renewed © 1963 by the Oswald Chambers Publications Assn. Ltd. Used by permission of Discovery House Publishers, Box 3566, Grand Rapids, MI 4950l. All rights reserved (pages 74, 87).

Reprinted with the permission of Scribner, an imprint of Simon & Schuster Adult Publishing Group, from *The Cost of Discipleship* by Dietrich Bonhoeffer. Copyright © 1959 by SCM Press Ltd. (pages 83-84, 98).

Taken from *Purpose-Driven® Life, The* by Rick Warren. Copyright © 2002 by Rick Warren. Used by permission of The Zondervan Corporation (page 85).

Taken from *Grace for the Moment* by Max Lucado. Copyright © 2000 by Max Lucado. Used by permission of J. Countryman, a division of Thomas Nelson, Inc. (pages 88-89).

Taken from *From Grey to Gold* by Marta Berg. Copyright © 1995 by Marta Berg. BCB Books. Used by permission (page 96).

Taken from *Growing Spiritually* by E. Stanley Jones. Copyright © MCMLIII by Pierce & Washabaugh. Used by permission of Abingdon Press (pages 103-104).

Taken from by an article in the ELCA publication, *The Lutheran* by Mark Hanson, Bishop. Used by permission of Mark Hanson and *The Lutheran* magazine 108-109).

In Public Domain

"Just As I Am", page 101

*I pay tribute to the unknown
authors of stories and
illustrations which could not be
traced to the proper source.
I apologize for any such instances.
If you recognize an uncited story,
please let me know and the
publisher and I will be sure to
acknowledge the author
in future printings.*

Other Books by William E. Berg

for more information visit **www.bergbooks.com**

Show Me the Way to Go Home
Journey to the Promised Land

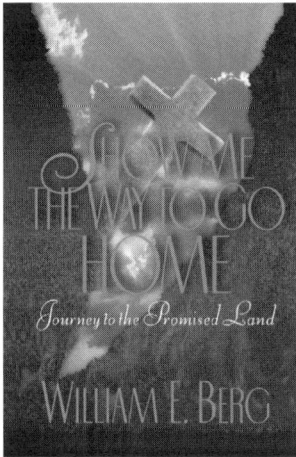

In this book, the author reminds us that the more heavenly-minded we are, the more practical our service will be in our Lord's work of healing and reconciliation in our broken world. He seeks to follow the Word of God Travel Service with Jesus Christ as Companion and Rescuer, and the Holy Sprit as Guide.

A Strange Thing Happened to Me on the Way to Retirement—I Never Arrived!

At the age of 90, the author in this book seeks to redefine retirement. He insists that there is no retirement policy in the Kingdom of God. Difficult choices and impairments of body and spirit in older age are recognized. The divine dimension of life as revealed in the Word of God is highlighted.

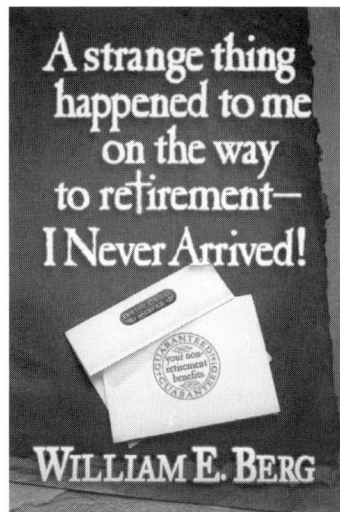

Prayer in the Name of Jesus
and Other Writings

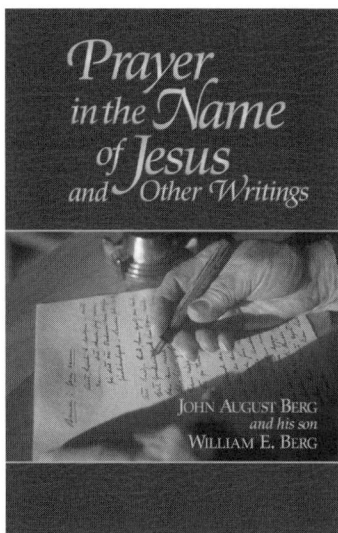

This book contains dramatic messages and stories from the lives of John A. Berg and his son, William E. Berg. John August Berg loved to walk. Walking and running with our Lord is the story of Amazing Grace and also the story of this book. Indeed, prayer is walking and talking with our Lord.

It's Okay Not to be Okay IF...

This is a book on the study of the *"Divine If's"*. The author wrote this book not least as a safeguard against the theology of cheap grace. Our God honors us with the priceless gifts of accountability and responsibility. He writes of the love of God which provides incentive and power to respond to His conditions.

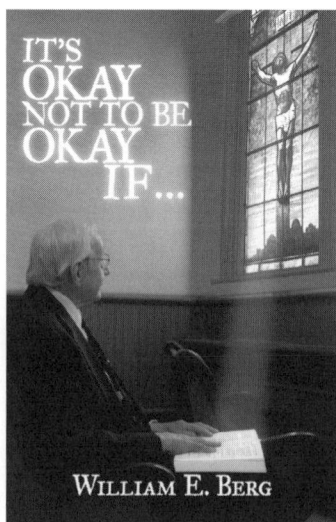